MEMPHIS

MEMPHIS

MURDER & MAYHEM

TERESA R. SIMPSON

Charleston ||H|| London

THE
History
PRESS

Published by The History Press
Charleston, SC 29403
www.historypress.net

First published 2008

Manufactured in the United States

ISBN 978.1.59629.521.6

Library of Congress Cataloging-in-Publication Data

Simpson, Teresa.
Memphis murder and mayhem / Teresa Simpson.
p. cm.
Includes bibliographical references (p.   ).
ISBN 978-1-59629-521-6
1. Murder--Tennessee--Memphis--History. 2. Murder--Tennessee--Memphis--Case studies.
3. Memphis (Tenn.)--Social conditions. I. Title.
HV6534.M4S57 2008
364.152'30976819--dc22
                    2008024601

This one is for Maya, who was with me every step of the way.

Contents

Acknowledgements

This book would not have been possible without the helpful contributions of so many. I would like to first thank my editor, John Wilkinson, who not only suggested this project to me, but also provided guidance and encouragement throughout.

A huge thank-you goes to Michael Finger, senior editor of *Memphis* magazine. He generously shared his research and insight into several of the stories that appear in this book. He is a wonderful writer and I am humbled by his gracious assistance.

I am deeply indebted to Andy Carter of the Memphis Public Library who aided in the inclusion of many of the beautiful and historic photos in this book.

I am also grateful to my husband, Michael J. Simpson, who is not only my partner in life, but has turned out to be a great research assistant as well.

There are a number of other people who offered their time, knowledge and talents to this project. These fabulous folks include Foster Bunday, Ed Frank, Paul V. Isbell, Jim Little, Robert J. McNamara, Chris Ratcliff, Tomás N. Romero and Amie Vanderford.

And, as always, I want to thank my family and friends for their support and encouragement.

Introduction

In the southwest corner of Tennessee, situated right on the bluffs of the mighty Mississippi River, is the city of Memphis. It boasts a population of nearly 650,000 and is proud to be called the "City of Good Abode." Memphis is known and appreciated for many things. It is lauded for its Southern hospitality and admired for its rich cultural background. It is the birthplace of the blues and it is America's Distribution Center. And of course, Memphis was home to the king—Elvis Presley.

In addition to the things that make the city great, Memphis has also had its fair share of trials and tribulations. During the Civil War, both the Union and Confederate armies fought for control of Memphis. The yellow fever epidemic in the 1870s nearly wiped out the city's population. In the 1960s, racial tensions and the struggle for civil rights came to a tragic head with the assassination of Dr. Martin Luther King Jr. But perhaps the longest enduring struggle that Memphis has had to face has been with violent crime.

Though certainly not the beginning of the city's war on crime, the birth of the Memphis Police Department in 1827 made that war an official one. In the very beginning, a single man named John Balch was the entirety of the force, having been named town constable. In a few years, two additional men were hired to keep watch over the city at night. Soon, an official police station was built at the corner of Main and Market Streets.

By the end of the nineteenth century, the police force had grown to one hundred men and had been reorganized to make patrols more efficient. In the early 1900s, the city bought its first patrol wagon, nicknamed the "Black Maria." In spite of these advancements in local law enforcement, violent crime was on the rise. By 1914, an article in the *New York Times* had dubbed Memphis the most violent city in America, citing the city's murder rate at 72.2 per 100,000 of population. In contrast, New York City had a murder rate of 6.1 per 100,000. As bad as things were in Memphis, they were only going to get worse.

The "Black Maria," Memphis's first police wagon. *Memphis and Shelby County Room, Memphis Public Library & Information Center.*

The police department did what it could to keep up with the growing crime problem in the city and continued to make advancements, including another reorganization of the force and the installation of two-way radios in the patrol vehicles. In 1925, the mayor of Memphis even convened the Memphis Crime Commission in an effort to determine the cause of the city's crime woes and to try to find ways to resolve them. Still, the crime rate was growing faster than the police could get a handle on it. In 1932, 102 murders were reported in Memphis. This number gave Memphis a new dubious distinction. No longer was our city just the most violent in America—it was now named Murder Capital of the World.

The late 1930s and the 1940s brought dramatic changes to the police force. The Police Academy was opened in 1937 by an officer who had graduated from the FBI National Academy. This, of course, led to a better-trained police force. Also during this time period, the workweek of a typical officer was reduced from forty-eight to forty hours. In 1948, the first African American police officers were hired. The force was also growing by leaps and bounds. By the end of the 1940s, the department had acquired a total of 471 employees and 108 police vehicles.

From there, crime rates in the city—although still high by comparison to other cities—were beginning to stabilize. Nonetheless, the police department continued to make strides by adding new technology, programs and initiatives on a regular basis. Some of these additions included the implementation of a neighborhood watch program, the opening of several new precincts and the creation of new units. All of these measures have aided in the city's fight against crime, but none of them has solved the problem completely.

Today, the police department employs more than two thousand officers, operates nine precincts and handles more than 800,000 calls per year—all in an effort to reduce crime throughout the city. Still, Memphis frequently tops the violent crime lists of various crime studies, including those compiled by the FBI. When it comes to murder alone, Memphis generally ranks in the top five or ten, falling behind crime-ridden cities such as Detroit, Washington, D.C., and Philadelphia. Memphis is, without a doubt, home to an unfortunate amount of murder.

From the sudden crimes of passion that occur with all-too-frequent regularity to the tragedies like the Lester Street massacre that shake us to our cores, we hear stories of murder and mayhem in the city on an almost daily basis. We commonly blame the high crime rate on the declining state of society as a whole. We seem to feel that people are becoming more depraved with each passing year. In Memphis, however, this is not a valid argument. In the pages ahead, you will read about some of the most shocking and scandalous murders of the nineteenth and twentieth centuries.

Due to the sheer number of recorded murders in our city's history, it was difficult to choose which of these cases should be included in the book. After all, there is no one victim who is more important than another, nor is there any one death more senseless than another. Nevertheless, I tried to choose murders that had a profound effect on Memphis, either at the time at which they occurred or beyond. Some of these crimes shocked the city simply because of the social prominence of the people involved. Others had scandalous circumstances surrounding them, causing a stir all over town. Then there were the murders that had an impact on our society as a whole by changing the way we thought or lived, or by shattering our illusions of innocence. To be sure, the effects of every one of these crimes could be felt by the people left behind. But some of them have changed all of our lives forever.

As you embark upon this journey through Memphis's troubled past, I hope you will also keep in mind the things that make this city a beautiful place to visit and live. Remember that murder and mayhem exist everywhere. These are just our stories.

Chapter 1

The Race Riot
of 1866

At the start of the Civil War, Memphis was greatly valued by the Confederate army and greatly coveted by the Union army due to its prime location and efficient transportation systems. The city served as a military supply depot for the Confederacy until the Union victory at Shiloh on April 7, 1862. In the summer of that year, Memphis became the Union headquarters for General Ulysses S. Grant.

As a Union territory, Memphis attracted a large number of former slaves, and the city's black population quadrupled from 1860 to 1870. After the war, this growing population enjoyed new freedoms and made great strides both socially and politically. In spite of this progress, some whites were still unable to embrace the idea of racial equality, and race relations were often strained. This strain was made evident in May 1866, when a race riot broke out, resulting in the cruel and senseless deaths of dozens. This riot was, without a doubt, one of the darkest chapters in Memphis's history.

Although perspectives varied, most accounts report that the trouble started with a group of soldiers stationed at Fort Pickering in downtown Memphis. These soldiers, part of the Third United States Colored Infantry, had been discharged and were awaiting payment. Their days were long and monotonous and they had little to do but wait. The soldiers began coming up with creative ways to pass the time, but some of them resorted to drinking. As a result, the infantry soon collectively gained a negative reputation, and the authorities were quick to take action against the soldiers for any seemingly small infraction.

On the afternoon of May 1, 1866, a group of these soldiers was walking down South Street, presumably drunk. They were loud and rowdy and were soon approached by police officers, who ordered them to settle down and disperse. Uninhibited due to their drunken states, some of the men began talking back in a belligerent manner. Two of the soldiers were promptly

THE CAMP OF THE CONTRABANDS ON THE BANKS OF THE MISSISSIPPI

A sketch of Fort Pickering, 1862. *Memphis and Shelby County Room, Memphis Public Library & Information Center.*

ERING, MEMPHIS, TENN.—From a Sketch by our Special Artist, Mr. Henri Lovie

1862

arrested. A few of the remaining soldiers decided to try to intervene on behalf of their detained comrades, and pandemonium quickly ensued. The soldiers and the police officers began shouting at one another and, eventually, fists began to fly. It is unclear who first pulled a gun, but at some point a pistol was fired and two of the officers were hit.

In consideration of the rumors that would soon be going around, it is important to mention the nature of the injuries that the police officers received. One officer was struck by a bullet in the hand and quickly recovered. The other was shot in the thigh and later died. Though the official report stated that the policeman was shot by rioters, some accounts maintain that the officer accidentally discharged his own weapon into his leg while trying to unholster it.

By the time police headquarters was notified of the situation, the stories were already growing wildly out of control and the incident was portrayed to be even grimmer than it already was. For this reason, the entire Memphis police force was deployed to the scene. As the policemen made their way to South Street, a number of white citizens who had heard about the commotion joined the procession. Many of these men were armed. At the same time, a number of black citizens arrived on the scene in support of the soldiers. Many of them were also armed. When the two groups came face to face, they were nearly equal in number, and neither was prepared to back down.

Although it is indisputable that a gunfight broke out between the two mobs, it is at this junction in the story that accounts differ wildly. At the time of the incident, it was widely reported that the first shots were fired by the group of black soldiers and citizens. Later, that point would be disputed when others alleged that it was the group of white police officers and citizens who fired first. In the aftermath of the event, this point seems irrelevant. Regardless of who opened fire, the result was bloody and tragic. By the end of the firefight, one white had been killed and five had been injured, while thirteen blacks had been killed and sixteen wounded.

The immediate reports coming out of Memphis painted a biased and inaccurate tale. The story was that soldiers from Fort Pickering had killed several police officers who were attempting to arrest one of the soldiers. Based on that partial and erroneous story, Union General George Stoneman ordered all of the soldiers to the barracks and confiscated their weapons. While the general undoubtedly believed this was in the best interest of all concerned, this move left black settlements in the area open and vulnerable to the mobs of angry whites that would soon form.

On the evening of May 1, stories of the afternoon's firefight began to spread through the city—many of them resembling in content the same story that was relayed to General Stoneman. As can be expected, the stories grew even more and more exaggerated with each telling. For the white citizens who were already getting worked up about the afternoon's events, these tales just added fuel to the fire and sparked renewed anger and resentment. To make matters worse, the city recorder, a man named John Creighton, further incited violence in a speech he made while standing at the corner of Vance and Causey Streets. Observers who attended the speech reported that Creighton urged white men to "go ahead and kill every damned one of the nigger race and burn up the cradle." It was further reported by witnesses that the recorder claimed to be "in favor of killing every God damned nigger."[1] Spurred on by rumors and encouragement from public officials such as Creighton, the violence grew more brutal as the night progressed.

After dark, an angry mob of whites congregated at the scene of the earlier fight and began firing their weapons at every black individual they could see. Without the soldiers there to protect them, most of the black population was helpless. The victims of these senseless shootings included men, women and children. In at least one instance, the lifeless body of a victim was brutalized further when it was shot multiple times, beaten and cut up. With good reason, most black citizens retreated into their homes and prayed for a swift end to the violence. According to most credible reports, there were no attacks on whites by blacks that evening.

In spite of the fact that the blacks had not provoked the situation further, a white mob again descended upon South Memphis on the morning of May 2. Once again, false rumors seemed to be the white mob's driving force. Due to a story going around that suggested that two white men had been killed the night before, the whites again proceeded to fire upon any black whom they ran across. In addition to these horrendous crimes, others were being committed in the area as well. Black women were being raped. The homes of black families were being looted and burned.

Although police officers made up a portion of the mob, one has to wonder why there was no intervention by any other person of authority. The mayor of Memphis, John Park, was reported to be in a state of intoxication at the time of the riots and was therefore incapable of doing anything to stop them. Shelby County Sheriff P.M. Minters claimed that he tried to calm the mob but that his attempts were unsuccessful, particularly as the mob's anger grew. Brigadier General Benjamin Runkle of the U.S. Army even made an appearance at one of the riots, but he admitted that he was unable to stop the mob; nor did he have any troops to offer backup support. Did these officials truly make an effort to bring peace to the streets of Memphis, or were they simply too cowardly to intervene? Either way, for all intents and

A sketch depicting the race riot of 1866. *Memphis and Shelby County Room, Memphis Public Library & Information Center.*

purposes, the city of Memphis was seized by mob rule during these first two days of May.

Finally, a group of army regulars arrived on the scene and managed to restore some order. The mob was dispersed and the shooting ceased. It seemed that the riots were over. After nightfall, however, the mob made a final and devastating statement by setting fire to numerous buildings and homes. As fire erupted throughout the city, many citizens voiced their approval. By the end of the night, four churches (including the oldest church in Memphis at the time), eight schoolhouses and ninety-one homes, complete with personal possessions, had been torched. These establishments were all owned or frequented primarily by blacks. In addition, it was reported that members of the mob, particularly police officers, took money from victims, some of whom had just been paid by the army. In monetary terms, the cost of the riot exceeded $100,000, a sizable sum in 1866.

The greatest cost, however, was the loss of human life and dignity. At least forty-six blacks and two whites were killed during the riot. Additionally, at least seventy-five others were injured, and five women were raped.

Before the month's end, a congressional committee was appointed to investigate the incident. This committee spent more than two weeks investigating the riots, questioning 170 witnesses and recording over two thousand pages of testimony. Their findings, which detailed the riot's horrors, helped the move toward Radical Reconstruction. During this phase of Reconstruction, the Republicans in Congress took charge of Reconstruction policies and even passed constitutional amendments in direct opposition to President Johnson. One such radical change implemented by the Republicans was the ratification of the Fourteenth Amendment, which guaranteed citizenship and federal civil rights to all persons born in the United States.

It is unfortunate that it took incidents such as the Memphis Race Riot of 1866 to help bring about such dramatic change. However, this was certainly not the first time, nor would it be the last time, that a great law has been born of hindsight rather than by the progressive thinking of lawmakers.

Chapter 2

His Daughter's Honor

For well over one hundred years, Seessel's was a household name in the Memphis area. This dry goods turned grocery store was considered by many to be the finest such chain in town and served generations of Memphis shoppers. Even today, the idea of murder occurring in such an innocuous location seems unlikely. In 1871, however, one Seessel's store became the scene of a scandalous crime that shocked the city.

At ten o'clock on the morning of August 29, a man named J.W.S. Browne walked into Seessel's carrying his double-barreled shotgun slung over his shoulder. Initially, no one questioned or detained him in any way. Perhaps it was perfectly acceptable to enter a store with a weapon in 1871. Or perhaps the rest of his attire put the store clerks at ease. Newspaper accounts at the time said that Browne was "dressed plainly, as a farmer." Maybe a farmer—even one carrying a shotgun—seemed harmless enough to most people. Another possibility is that Browne was recognized upon entering the store. As a newspaperman and respected citizen of Memphis, it is unlikely that anyone would have thought twice about the shotgun. Whatever the reason, the man was able to walk into the store with a loaded shotgun and no one asked any questions.

Mr. Browne approached the counter and asked a clerk to see some lawns, a type of finely woven, light cotton fabric. The clerk, a man named Beasley, quickly obliged this request. After he had spent a moment examining the fabrics, Mr. Brown asked to see some linens. Mr. Beasley told his customer that the linens were kept in the back of the store and began leading the way. As an apparent afterthought, he paused for just a moment and asked if Mr. Browne would prefer to keep his shotgun at the front of the store. Mr. Browne quickly assured him that he did not mind carrying the weapon and would keep it with him. The store clerk had phrased his question in such a way to suggest that he was merely trying to be accommodating to his

Seessel's dry goods store. *Memphis and Shelby County Room, Memphis Public Library & Information Center.*

customer. Nevertheless, it seems plausible that Mr. Beasley was growing a bit apprehensive about walking to the rear of the store with an armed man. As time would soon tell, he had reason for apprehension.

As the pair reached the back of the store, Browne could see that one counter was being attended by Captain J. Theodore Adams. Adams was assisting two ladies who were inspecting some fabrics. As Beasley and Browne passed by the ladies, Beasley turned around to check on his customer and witnessed a startling scene. Mr. Browne, with his shotgun perched upon his shoulder, was taking aim at Adams. Before Browne had a chance to fire, Adams saw the gun pointed toward him and immediately dropped behind the counter, attempting to take refuge behind some boxes. Undeterred, Mr. Browne ran to the end of the counter, where he had a clear shot of Adams, and began firing. Buckshot spewed from Browne's weapon and entered Adams's only leg just below the knee. The buckshot shattered the bone and severed the femoral artery.

Adams lay on the floor, crying out in pain, as he struggled to retrieve his own revolver. He cried out, "Don't shoot! For God's sake, somebody take him away!"[2]

By then, Browne had calmly walked out of the store and handed his weapon to someone standing outside. That person was not identified, but was presumed to be an accomplice, possibly Browne's son, John. He then . walked directly to the police station nearby, where he met Memphis Police Captain Athey. Browne said to Athey, "I wish to surrender myself. I shot a man in Seessel's store a few minutes ago and I guess I killed him."[3]

Back at Seessel's, store employees were attending to Adams's wounds and had called for a wagon to transport Adams back to his boardinghouse. A pair of doctors met him at the home and examined the wound. This medical assistance had arrived too late, however, and J. Theodore Adams bled to death shortly after 1:00 p.m.

When the proverbial smoke had cleared, local residents were baffled. What would have prompted a respected pressman and citizen to calmly and deliberately shoot down another man in cold blood? In the aftermath of the murder, the scandalous story leading up to the shooting became clear.

It seems that Captain Adams had been pursuing Browne's daughter Millie for some time. The two went to First Baptist Church together, but were introduced by Millie's sister. While Millie was relatively receptive to his attentions, it was important to her that the two of them take things slowly and properly. Adams, on the other hand, was constantly pushing for more and gave every indication that he was interested in a physical relationship. During this era, such a relationship was not socially acceptable, to say the least, and Millie resisted. Ever persistent, Adams finally asked Millie to marry him. Whether he ever had any intention of marrying the girl is unknown. Millie, on the other hand, had fallen in love with the young captain and did have every intention of marrying him. Nonetheless, she felt that it was too soon to accept a marriage proposal and asked him to give her more time.

Things were not working out quite the way Adams planned, and so he tried yet another tactic. Already knowing the answer, he asked Millie if her father was a Mason. When she answered affirmatively, Adams told her that he, too, was a Mason and that Masons had a duty to look after each other's families. It was therefore right and proper, he went onto explain, that the two should become engaged. Accepting his reasoning, Millie finally also accepted his marriage proposal. It must have been easier to seduce a woman once engaged to her, for shortly thereafter, the relationship was consummated. When asked later why she allowed herself to be seduced, Millie said, "I considered him in the light of my future husband. I loved him, he expressed his great love for me, kissed me, caressed me, and in an unguarded moment I yielded."[4]

Just a few weeks later, Millie discovered that she was pregnant. When she told her fiancé about her condition, he instructed her to keep it quiet, but made vague promises about marrying her when he had more money. She assured him that she would do her best to keep her condition hidden. In time, of course, that became impossible and Millie went back to Adams and told him that there was no way for her to keep her condition hidden much longer. She pleaded with him to just go ahead and marry her. At that, Adams told Millie that he was still financially unable to take a wife. He further said that if she revealed his identity to anyone, their relationship would be over. Although their relationship was virtually nonexistent by this point, Millie vowed to keep his identity a secret.

Soon the young woman had no choice but to tell her father that she was pregnant. He demanded to know who the father of the baby was, but Millie refused over and over again to tell him. In desperation, she wrote several letters to her fiancé, begging him to come and marry her, but she received no response. Rejected and alone, Millie finally told her father that it was Theodore Adams who was the father of her child.

The very next morning, Mr. Browne went to Seessel's. There, he confronted Captain Adams, demanding that the young man marry his daughter. Adams asked Browne to leave the store, but agreed to meet him later at ten thirty. When Adams failed to show up, the angry father returned to Seessel's, where he found his daughter's seducer working behind the counter. Adams maintained that another employee had taken ill and he had therefore been unable to leave the shop. He then asked Browne to meet him around the corner. Browne, together with his son, did meet Adams at a location on Union Avenue. It was there that Captain Adams told Browne that he was unable to marry Millie because he did not have any money. Undeterred, the father offered to help the young couple financially and assured Adams that Millie was willing to marry him. Having no legitimate arguments left, Adams flatly refused to marry the girl.

Mr. Browne was furious at this and vowed, "I will go unarmed today, but if you do not marry my daughter this day, you take your own life in your hand."

Adams apparently did not take the threat seriously as he laughed and told Browne that he could just as easily pull a gun on the other man.

Overnight, Mr. Browne continued to stew about the situation, telling some of his relatives that he intended to kill Adams. As it was, Browne did not even own a gun of his own and had to rent one from a man, using the excuse that he was going hunting. Instead, he walked into Seessel's store and killed the man who had "ruined" his daughter.

In making his confession to the police, Browne frequently stopped and wept. It seems that Mr. Browne was a man driven by his own moral code. He couldn't accept the fact that his daughter's virtue had been sullied, and he considered her ruined, a common mentality during that era. By the same token, he had great difficulty in accepting the fact that he had taken another man's life.

Most people, it seemed, believed that Browne's actions were both warranted and honorable. One grand jury after another refused to indict him on the charge of murder. Finally, the prosecutor was able to secure an indictment after presenting the case to a fourth grand jury. Though indicted for the crime, Browne was never convicted.

As for Millie Browne, she managed to get past the stigma of having been "ruined." She was married to Mr. William Bell in 1873, less than two years after the murder of her first fiancé.

Chapter 3

Murder at the Peabody

The Peabody Hotel is arguably the finest hotel in Memphis and stands as an emblem, not only of the city, but also of the South as a whole. The hotel that sits on Union Avenue today, however, is not the original Peabody. The original Peabody Hotel was built in 1869 at the corner of Main and Monroe Streets. It was built by Colonel Robert C. Brinkley and was named after his newly deceased friend, George Peabody. The original structure boasted seventy-five rooms, a ballroom and a saloon. Like today's hotel, the original was also considered to be among the finest in the South.

On December 4, 1886, a twenty-two-year-old man named Russell Godwin (who was the son of a prominent local banker) walked into the lobby of this fine hotel. He walked directly to the registration desk and browsed through the names in the registration book. Apparently not finding what he was looking for, he turned around to leave.

Just as Russell Godwin began to walk away, he spotted the very person for whom he was searching—twenty-four-year-old Thomas Dalton. Mr. Dalton was sitting in a chair in the Peabody's rotunda, leisurely passing the time as he was currently unemployed. Upon seeing Dalton, Godwin stopped and pulled a revolver from his hip pocket. He immediately fired one shot at Dalton, hitting him in the chest. When Dalton fell to the ground, Godwin walked up to the man and fired three more shots at him. Dalton's death was so instantaneous that not even a groan was heard by any of the witnesses. Godwin then set his gun on a cigar stand on the rotunda and walked right out the front door, where he was promptly arrested.

Upon his arrest, Godwin refused to make a statement to authorities, yet rumors were already spreading rapidly as to why this son of a prominent family would commit such an act. It seemed that Mr. Dalton had been telling tales that could potentially tarnish the reputation of Godwin's married sister, Annie, wife of Mr. John Polk. As in the case of the murder

The original Peabody Hotel in 1888. *Memphis and Shelby County Room, Memphis Public Library & Information Center.*

at Seessel's, a tarnished reputation could certainly have justified murder in the minds of some.

Annie and Thomas met in 1883, two years after Annie's marriage to John Polk. The Polks had just moved from Bolivar to live with Annie's parents in a house on Elliot Street in Memphis. Thomas Dalton lived next door to the Godwins with his widowed mother. At the time they met, Thomas was recovering from a serious illness, the nature of which is now unknown. Due to his illness, Annie Polk took a neighborly interest in the young man and checked on him frequently. Through the course of his illness and recovery, Annie's interest went from a neighborly one to a romantic one. These feelings were reciprocated by Thomas, and the two began spending a great deal of time with each other. Annie would put on a veil as a disguise and the two would go riding together. At other times, Annie invited Thomas into her home when no one else was present. When Thomas's mother began to realize the nature of her son's relationship with Annie, she wrote a letter to the young woman asking her to leave Thomas alone. "If not for your own sake," Mrs. Dalton wrote, "at least for your mother's." Mrs. Dalton also threatened to tell Annie's husband about the affair if she did not end it immediately.

Annie was unimpressed by this threat and showed the letter to Thomas. He was angry that his mother was meddling in his business and he promptly tore up the letter in front of her. This incident drove a wedge between mother and son.

Mrs. Dalton was not the only one writing letters, however. At Mr. Godwin's trial, several letters written in Annie's hand and addressed to Thomas were presented before the court. Although Annie denied having written them, witnesses recognized as handwriting experts testified that Annie was, indeed, the author of the letters. With that, there was no denying that an affair had really been going on, a point that had been disputed until then—at least by Annie.

Thomas Dalton, on the other hand, seemed to enjoy telling others about his purported relationship with a married woman. Soon, Mrs. Polk's reputation suffered. This not only hurt Annie, but also reflected badly on her husband and the entire Godwin family. Of course, Annie really was carrying on inappropriately with Thomas and so she was as much to blame for her tarnished reputation as he.

Aside from gossiping about his affair, Thomas proved to be something of an unscrupulous character. After his relationship with Annie ended, the young man thought he might be able to make a little money from the experience and decided to blackmail Annie's father, Mr. John Godwin. Thomas had the letters from Annie in his possession—the very ones later used in court to prove the affair. He threatened to make the letters public if John Godwin didn't pay Thomas for them. Godwin ultimately paid Dalton $100 to destroy the letters, but then promptly reported the blackmail to police. In an effort to avoid prosecution, Dalton fled from Memphis and headed to St. Louis.

When he reappeared in Memphis three months later, Russell Godwin got wind of the fact that he had returned. Frustrated for his family—particularly his father and sister—Russell decided to rid his family of the problem once and for all and tracked Dalton down at his favorite haunt, the Peabody Hotel.

On December 8, Godwin was arraigned on the charge of murder. Although he pled not guilty, he was soon indicted for his crime. Due to his high social prominence, his attorneys asked that Godwin be placed under special guard instead of being thrown in with the rest of the prison population. The judge refused and sent him back to jail, where he would spend the next two months.

On January 24, 1887, Russell Godwin's trial began. While the defense presented evidence showing that Thomas Dalton had been something of a cad, the prosecution called witnesses that made Annie Polk out to be something of a jezebel. In particular, Dalton's mother and aunt testified that they often saw provocative behavior on Annie's part and suggested that Dalton had been an innocent boy until he met the married woman.

The trial lasted until February 14, when the jury began its deliberations. In spite of the testimony showing that Annie was equally responsible for the affair, most people—the jury included—seemed to feel that Dalton must have been the seducer and Annie merely his victim. The next day, the jury returned with a verdict of not guilty.

The case was reported to be one of Memphis's most sensational murders. This was primarily because the people involved, both killer and victim, were members of the city's high society. Add to that the scandalous nature of an extramarital affair and you have a crime that captivates the interest of the general public—particularly in 1886. An 1887 article in the *New York Times* said it best:

> *The trial occupied 20 days, and from the amount of filth unearthed, the prominence of the families concerned, and the ability of counsel on both sides, is regarded as one of the most famous in the history of the South.*[5]

The trial was complete and the verdict was returned, but this scandalous case reared its ugly head once more the following December. Two of the jurors came forward and accused jury foreman Frank Ozanne of bribery. Ozanne, a downtown storekeeper, had asserted during jury selection that he had formed no opinion on the case whatsoever. At some point along the way, either before or during the trial, Ozanne decided that Godwin should go free. Though it is possible that he truly believed Godwin to have been justified in the shooting, speculation at the time suggested that perhaps Godwin's family or other supporters had themselves bribed the foreman. This would have made it in his best interest to secure a not guilty verdict. Regardless of his motives, it is clear that he offered at least two of the jurors $1,000 each to vote for a not guilty verdict. For this, Ozanne was arrested and charged with bribery.

That development, of course, had no impact on Russell Godwin's legal status as he could not be tried twice for the same crime. In 1907, Russell Godwin died a free, but troubled man at the age of forty-two. The official cause of death was listed as alcoholism.

Chapter 4

Tainted Love

High society, forbidden love and insanity may sound like the makings of a modern-day soap opera, but in 1892, these were very real elements of one of the most scandalous murders in Memphis history.

The story begins with nineteen-year-old Alice Mitchell, the seventh child of a wealthy furniture dealer. Although the Mitchells were prominent in local society, the family quietly struggled with mental illness. Mrs. Mitchell, in fact, had spent some time in an insane asylum and allegedly suffered the most severe attacks of psychosis after childbirth. Additionally, one of Alice's brothers had suffered from "mental derangement" following a case of sunstroke, and she had several cousins who were purported to be insane.

Alice herself was considered to be odd by many standards. As a child, she was high-strung and, at times, cruel. She was known to do things such as suspend cats by one leg. As she grew older, both her physical development and academic progress were stunted to a degree. To make matters worse, she was somewhat unattractive and awkward. In spite of these peculiarities, it was the fact that Alice never exhibited an interest in boys or men that people would remember in years to come.

Though the girl was an outcast in many ways, Alice did have at least a couple of friends with whom she was particularly close. One of these friends, Freda Ward, was the daughter of family friends and was about the same age as Alice. The two girls had been close friends for many years, but at some point a different sort of relationship evolved and the girls fell in love.

While homosexuality is slowly becoming more accepted by society in the twenty-first century, it was virtually unheard of in 1892. Attraction to someone of the same sex was considered to be unnatural and the result of mental illness or deficiency. Alice Mitchell, however, seemed to be oblivious to this stigma, speaking freely of her love for the other woman. Freda, on the other hand, was far more secretive about the relationship. Though Alice would later deny that the two had a sexual relationship, witnesses reported seeing the girls kiss and hug in a way that was considered to be inappropriate.

When Alice and Freda were both eighteen years of age, the Ward family moved to Golddust, Tennessee, a small town sixty miles north of Memphis, where Freda's father, John, made his living as a wealthy planter and merchant. Though heartbroken by the new distance between them, the lovers continued their relationship via correspondence interspersed by occasional visits.

It was during one such visit that Alice grew convinced that Freda was showing an interest in two young men who had been flirting with her on the street. Overcome by jealousy, Alice took a high dose of laudanum, an opium derivative, and then tried to pour some down Freda's throat while the woman was sleeping. Freda woke up before ingesting the drug, but Alice became violently ill. While one might imagine that a murder/suicide attempt would have ended the relationship, it seemed to have the opposite effect on the two girls. They continued their correspondence with renewed passion. Before long, more madly in love than ever, Alice proposed marriage to Freda with an engagement ring.

While Alice understood that two women could not lawfully marry each other, she seemed to believe that they could marry if she simply pretended to be a man. In fact, Alice had the whole elopement plot planned out. She suggested that the two go to St. Louis under assumed names. Alice would dress in men's clothing and take a job to support the two of them. She even believed that she would be able to grow a mustache by shaving her upper lip repeatedly. In spite of the ludicrousness of the plan, Freda accepted Alice's proposal.

Before the women could run away to St. Louis together, however, Freda's family learned of the girls' intentions and returned the engagement ring to Alice's mother. Freda was then forbidden to have anything to do with Alice. Likewise, Alice was admonished by her own family to have no further interaction with Freda. Though perhaps not by choice, correspondence between the two girls ceased.

While Freda was seemingly content to get on with her life, Alice was completely devastated by these events and began to show signs of depression. She wouldn't eat, she grew listless and she lost weight. In addition, some of her behavior could best be described as manic; she would laugh hysterically one moment and burst into tears the next. This proved to be a turning point in the story.

Shortly after the girls' "breakup," Alice learned that Freda and her sister Jo would be in Memphis for several weeks as guests in the home of a widow who lived on Hernando Street. Having recently learned to drive a horse and buggy, Alice drove past the widow's home several times in hopes of spotting Freda. She would even park near the home just to catch a glimpse of Freda passing by a window.

Tainted Love

On January 25, 1892, the day the Ward sisters were scheduled to return to Golddust, Alice stole a razor from her father, silently resolving to kill Freda if the two could not be together. Alice then took her family's buggy to the home of her friend Lillie Johnson and invited her to come out for a ride. Lillie agreed and even brought her young nephew along. Alice drove straight to Hernando Street and lingered there, waiting for Freda. Freda, Jo and their friend Christina finally emerged from the home and began to make their way to the boat dock, where they would board the *Ora Lee*, a riverboat that would take them up the Mississippi River to Golddust.

As the three girls passed the buggy, Freda glanced at Alice but did not acknowledge her. Jo, in fact, had urged Freda to pass by Alice without a word. Alice followed the trio for a few moments before declaring to Lillie that she absolutely had to speak with Freda. She jumped out of the buggy and approached her former lover from behind, slashing the girl's throat with the razor. When Jo realized what Alice had done to her sister, she immediately began trying to fight off the attacker. Alice managed to cut Jo, too, resulting in a few superficial wounds. She then dashed back to the buggy, where she told Lillie what she had done. When she arrived at home, she also told her mother what had transpired. As she told the story, her attitude came across as matter-of-fact and unremorseful. Later, however, when she apparently realized what she had done, Alice broke down into hysterics, screaming and crying and kissing a photograph of Freda.

Meanwhile, a crowd had gathered around the Ward girls and some bystanders lifted Freda into a buggy that would transport her to a nearby doctor's office. The young woman died upon arrival at the doctor's office so she was transported to an undertaker. That very evening, a coroner's inquest was convened and Alice was charged with premeditated murder. Incidentally, Lillie Johnson was also charged with murder because the authorities believed her to be an accomplice to the crime. Though Alice initially refused to talk, she eventually made a startling statement:

> *I was in love with Freda. I could not live without her. Long ago we made a compact that if we were ever separated we should kill each other. When I found that Josie* [Freda's sister, Jo] *had forbidden Freda to have anything more to do with me I saw nothing else to do but to kill her. I took father's razor, but told no one what I was going to do.*[6]

Although Alice's statement indicated that Lillie was in no way involved in the planning or the commencement of the attack, the charges against her still stood.

The *Ora Lee*, a riverboat on the Mississippi. *Memphis and Shelby County Room, Memphis Public Library & Information Center.*

Alice's trial began on July 18. While on the witness stand, she described the murder dispassionately and with no visible remorse most of the time. She did have occasional outbursts of emotion, however, and shouted out proclamations such as "Freda has broken her faith!" and "I have killed her because I loved her so!" This behavior, along with the testimony of medical experts, indicated that Alice suffered from some form of mental illness.

On July 30, the jury was charged with determining whether Alice was sane or insane. Just twenty minutes later, the jury returned with this verdict: "We, the jury, find the defendant, Alice Mitchell, insane and believe it would endanger the safety of the community to set her at liberty."

From there, Ms. Mitchell was sent to the West Tennessee Hospital for the Insane in Bolivar, with the stipulation that should she ever be declared sane, she could then stand trial for Freda's murder. The judge assigned to preside

The West Tennessee Hospital for the Insane. *Memphis and Shelby County Room, Memphis Public Library & Information Center.*

over both Alice's and Lillie's trial put the matter on hold, stating that when Alice was released from the asylum, both girls could be tried together. Eight months later, all charges were dropped against Lillie Johnson as there was no evidence to prove her involvement in the crime.

In October of that year, it seemed that a trial for Alice was imminent, as reports out of Bolivar suggested that the woman was making great strides toward recovery. In spite of this optimistic prognosis, Alice's return to sanity did not occur, and in 1895, the woman attempted suicide. A doctor at the asylum discovered a suicide note next to Alice's bed one evening and found her on the roof of the hospital, wet but unharmed.

Based not on her sexual orientation, but rather on her peculiar actions and reactions, it seems likely that Alice Mitchell was mentally disturbed to some degree. Was she criminally insane? The jury seemed to think so and the murder case never went to trial. Alice died in 1898, still an inmate of the West Tennessee Hospital for the Insane.

Chapter 5

A Husband Scorned

In the early morning hours of May 19, 1900, a young servant woman named Ella Cummins was sleeping soundly in the back room of a house at 5 Jefferson Avenue, where she was employed by Mrs. Lillie Vadakin. Well before dawn, Ella was awakened suddenly by the sound of gunshots and a woman's screams. Terrified, Ella ran from the house without pausing to investigate the source of the commotion. She sought help from neighbors and the police were soon summoned.

When the police arrived at Mrs. Vadakin's home, they came upon a startling and scandalous scene. Lillie Vadakin, a married but separated woman, lay dead in her bed with a single gunshot wound to the chest. Lying next to her was the body of a man named Henry Reichman bearing three gunshot wounds—two to the chest and one to the center of the forehead. There was no indication that the home had been ransacked or that anything had been taken, effectively ruling out robbery as a motive. Instead, it appeared that this murder had been personal.

The police were baffled and plagued by several questions. Why would someone have come in and shot these two in cold blood? What was Henry Reichman doing in Lillie Vadakin's bed? And the most pressing question of all—where was *Mr.* Vadakin?

In 1900, such a scenario was surely far more scandalous than it would be today. In that year, fewer than 8 percent of marriages ended in divorce and extramarital affairs were not glamorized by soap operas and romance novels. And of course, murder was always a wicked affair, and certainly no more so than when it involved a love triangle. To determine if there really was a love triangle in play, the authorities had to uncover what had caused the breakdown of the Vadakins' marriage. From there, they had to ascertain whether this marital discord could possibly have driven Mr. Vadakin to murder.

The story began happily enough in 1886, when sixteen-year-old Lillie Landvoight moved with her family from Memphis to Forrest City, Arkansas. Lillie's father was a newspaper editor for the *Forrest City Times*, where he worked alongside another editor and manager of the paper, twenty-two-year-old Edward L. Vadakin. Edward was an ambitious young man who had almost single-handedly transferred the dying newspaper into a thriving one just months after he took a position there.

Shortly after the Landvoights moved to Arkansas, Lillie met Edward through her father and the two fell in love. After a whirlwind courtship, they were united in marriage in May 1886. Almost everyone who knew the couple seemed to be pleased for them and believed they would be quite happy together. The only person who expressed any concerns at all about the union was Lillie's sister, who felt that the two were rushing into marriage and might be making a mistake. It was speculated, though, that some of her protests were actually rooted in jealousy.

The general consensus seemed to be most accurate, as Edward and Lillie were, by all accounts, happy for the first several years of their marriage. Their finances were in good order and the newspaper was thriving. So successful was the newspaper venture, in fact, that Edward Vadakin and Edwin Landvoight purchased the *Forrest City Times* together, becoming business partners. Life at home was also good as the couple had four children together. Tragedy did strike in 1891, however, when the Vadakins' son, Edwin, died at one year and seven months of age. His cause of death is unknown.

Certainly a tragedy such as the death of a child can put a strain on the best of marriages. With this in mind, it is possible that their son's death marked the beginning of the end of their marriage. It was six years later that the couple was *known* to have some marital unhappiness, suggesting, perhaps, that it started some time earlier. Regardless of when it started, by 1898, things had gotten pretty bad in the Vadakin home. The couple was bickering constantly, and both Edward and Lillie were growing tired of their marriage. They mutually decided to separate.

Although there was no attempt at reconciliation, by all appearances it seemed that the separated Vadakins were getting along amicably. Edward and his father-in-law maintained their working relationship, and Lillie decided to return to her hometown of Memphis, at least on a temporary basis, and she soon moved into her Jefferson Street home. Edward made a brief trip to Memphis to file for divorce, hoping to avoid the publicity that would have surely ensued from a divorce in Forrest City, where he was well-known and respected. He sued for absolute divorce on unspecified statutory grounds on May 14, 1900. In light of the nature of the relationship, it

The marriage license issued to E.L Vadakin and Lillie Landvoigt. *Shelby County Archives.*

seems likely that these unspecified grounds were a century-old equivalent of today's irreconcilable differences. After all, the couple had been unable to get along, but there had been no reports of extramarital affairs, abuse or any other significant issue in the marriage.

In Memphis, Lillie and her servant girl lived alone, but on at least one occasion Lillie had an overnight guest in her home. On the evening of May 18, Lillie and Henry Reichman retired for the night—together. Mr. Reichman was a young man of only twenty-one years. He already had something of a bad reputation and was known to be a source of concern for his father. Henry had already been involved in multiple drunken brawls and had found himself mixed up in a few other petty crimes. Could the bad boy image have been what drew Lillie Vadakin to someone nine years her junior? And could outrage and jealousy of that relationship have caused a man to shoot his wife and her lover in cold blood?

The Memphis police seemed to think that was a plausible scenario and sent a request to Forrest City asking the authorities there to detain Edward Vadakin. The widower denied any involvement in the crime and, in fact, denied that he had ever left Forrest City. However, some witnesses actually reported seeing Vadakin in Memphis on the night of the murder and claimed that he returned to Forrest City on the midnight train. Vadakin was cooperative with the local police department, but refused to come to Memphis unless he was forced to do so by mandate of the authorities.

In 1900, just like today, the spouse of a murder victim is often the first suspect to whom police turn their attention. Certainly, the husband of a woman who is sleeping with another man would be considered a person of interest in a murder case. The police continued to investigate Edward Vadakin, questioning his story and tracking his whereabouts. Not only did they fail to turn up any real evidence against the man, but they were also left with one nagging question regarding motive. Why would a man who was divorcing his wife go into a jealous rage strong enough to drive him to murder? This question, along with the lack of evidence, was what ultimately spared Edward Vadakin from prison time or worse, for he was never convicted of the crime. In fact, just three years later, he went on to marry another woman named Grace Darling. The two of them had one child.

In spite of the certain controversy surrounding her death, Lillie Vadakin was remembered fondly by those who loved her. Her obituary in the *Forrest City Times* read:

> *In Memoriam—On Friday night, May 18, 1900, our friend Mrs. Lily [sic] B. Vadakin whom we had learned to love by years of association, for her many noble qualities was claimed by that grim destroyer, death, and her*

Edward Lincoln Vadakin. *Paul V. Isbell, Richmond, Virginia.*

earthly tabernacle became dissolved. Her history is written upon the eternal tablets of time; although not without blemishes, nor without faults, and transgressions, still brilliantly illuminated are some of the pages with many deeds of heroism, patience, gentleness and devotion, that constrains us to throw the mantle of charity over her shortcomings, remembering that "to err is human, to forgive divine." Her deeds of charity and benevolence which she dispensed in the years of her comparative affluence and happiness, relieving the sick and distressed, are glittering monuments to a soul which fate decreed to an early grave.

Interestingly enough, the children from Vadakin's marriage to Lillie went on to live with relatives in Shelbyville, Illinois. Did Vadakin feel ill-equipped to raise children on his own or was it deemed more appropriate that the children live with his aunt and uncle because they were a married couple of child-bearing age that could provide a stable home for them? Or, is it possible that certain family members *did* suspect Edward's involvement in the murders and therefore urged him to send the children away, ultimately for their own protection and well-being?

It seems clear that at least one relative did not suspect that Vadakin was a killer. Lillie's own father, Edwin Landvoight, remained Vadakin's partner at the *Forrest City Times* until Vadakin's death in 1915. He was fifty years old.

No one was ever convicted in the death of Lillie Vadakin or Henry Reichman. Likewise, no records can be found indicating that there was ever a suspect considered other than Edward Vadakin. If justice was ever served in the case, it was not here in this earthly realm.

Chapter 6

Murder by Mail

It was an ordinary day in May 1903, when a murderer-to-be walked into a Memphis drugstore and purchased a measure of arsenic. The poison-wielding individual then headed to a nearby saloon and obtained a bottle of whiskey. After carefully mixing the arsenic into the whiskey, the villain headed down to a neighborhood shop and obtained a pasteboard box in which to pack the bottle. From there, the package with the bottle was taken down to the local Adams Express station, addressed to its intended victim and put on a train for Cincinnati.

The facts of the story to this point are indisputable. It is when placing the blame that some conjecture and speculation must come into play as there is no record of anyone ever having been convicted of the crime. On the other hand, there is no record of the prime suspect ever having been cleared, either. For this reason, the rest of the story will be presented as it *allegedly* happened.

Lizzie McCormick was a thirty-year-old housekeeper who lived and worked in Memphis. Though she was married, she and her husband had been estranged for many months. For some time, she had been employed in the home of Mr. Edward Pell, a man who ran a local saloon. The two became close, but the relationship was not a romantic one—at least not for Edward. Lizzie, on the other hand, was growing increasingly affectionate toward her boss and resented him giving his attentions to any other woman—including his own relatives.

Lizzie had particularly become concerned about Edward's relationship with his sister-in-law, Kate Nobbe, who lived in Cincinnati. Though Lizzie and Kate had once been friendly with one another, Lizzie's resentment soon put an end to that. She began sending letters to the Cincinnati woman, threatening her and warning her to leave Edward alone. Kate, however, was not having an affair with her brother-in-law and tried to dismiss the jealous woman's threats.

In the spring of 1903, Edward had paid a visit to Kate and her family and had spent a couple of weeks there. This enraged Lizzie and she began brainstorming ways to remove Kate Nobbe from her life and, more importantly, from the life of Edward Pell. Soon, she had a diabolical plan in mind and she set off for the drugstore to put her plan into motion.

On the afternoon of May 13, several employees of Adams Express were unloading packages from a train car in Cincinnati. As fate would have it, one of the packages dropped and broke, quickly revealing that its contents were alcoholic in nature. The employees, not wanting to waste perfectly good whiskey, poured the remaining liquid into a container and five of them drank from it. Just a few short moments later, the men began to have violent reactions from drinking the lethal mixture. One of the men who was still able to function ran to get a doctor. Upon his arrival, the doctor was easily able to determine that the men had been poisoned by arsenic. Though an antidote was immediately given, one man, John Benjamin Ficker, died en route to the hospital. Three more were in critical condition but would eventually recover. The fifth man, who had drunk far less of the poison, quickly recovered without complication.

The Cincinnati police were immediately called in to investigate the package. They found that it had been addressed to Kate Nobbe of Cincinnati and that it had originated in Memphis. The police took the suspicious package to Mrs. Nobbe, who immediately identified the handwriting on the outside. It belonged, she said, to Lizzie McCormick. Kate further told the police of the bizarre circumstances surrounding Kate's relationship with Lizzie. She explained to investigators that Lizzie was "intensely jealous"[7] and produced the threatening letters from Lizzie as evidence.

This was enough evidence that the police felt an investigation into Lizzie's past was warranted. They soon learned that Lizzie had a jealous side. In the last several years, she had been involved in three other instances in which she was jealous of a woman because of the attention she was receiving from a particular man. In each of these situations, some sort of criminal behavior ensued and Lizzie was arrested. No charges were ever brought against her, though—at least not until May 1903.

From there, the police discovered that the pasteboard box in which the poisoned whiskey had been sent was obtained from a shop just down the street from Edward Pell's saloon. The shopkeeper's name was imprinted on the box, making it easily identifiable. The shopkeeper's wife went on to inform investigators that Lizzie had requested a box of that size and the wife obliged the request. Soon, they had also discovered that the very type of whiskey that was sent to Mrs. Nobbe could be found in Edward Pell's saloon.

With those facts as evidence, the Cincinnati authorities had little doubt as to who the murderer actually was and began pushing for Mrs. McCormick's arrest in Memphis. Memphis police quickly complied. Detectives from Cincinnati travelled to Memphis in hopes of bringing Lizzie back to their city, but the accused murderess refused to go to Cincinnati voluntarily. The detectives proceeded to question Lizzie, who grew agitated and tearful upon hearing the accusations that were being made against her. She claimed that after Edward Pell had returned from Cincinnati, Kate Nobbe had mailed a package to her that contained a candy baby. The implications of this were insulting to Lizzie and she asserted that she promptly returned it to Mrs. Nobbe. She maintained that the candy baby was the only thing she mailed to the other woman and suggested that the two packages had gotten mixed up. The investigators did not believe the woman and wanted to bring her back to Cincinnati to charge her with murder. Because of her refusal to go, however, the argument was heard before a judge, who ruled in her favor, saying that if a crime had been committed, it had been when Lizzie sent the poison—and that, of course, happened in Memphis. For that reason, Lizzie was charged with murder in Memphis and was remanded to the Shelby County Jail until her case could be presented to the grand jury. Meanwhile, Edward Pell vowed to provide his housekeeper with the best legal defense he could find.

By the end of the month, Lizzie's life was falling apart around her. She had been indicted in the murder of John Benjamin Ficker and was the target of scandalous rumors. Her husband had finally divorced her and, if that wasn't bad enough, eloped with Lizzie's fifteen-year-old sister. From there, the story of Lizzie McCormick grows cold. Records of a trial cannot be found, let alone of an outcome. After November 1903, there is no mention of Lizzie in the newspapers, nor can any marriage, birth or death record be found on the woman. It is as if the accused murderess just slipped away into oblivion.

Though there is no known record of Lizzie McCormick's conviction or acquittal, the murder remains one of Memphis's most intriguing, even a century after the fact. This is undoubtedly due to the nature of the criminal, a relatively young and attractive woman; the nature of the crime, a poisoning via mail; and the nature of the victim, an unintended target who happened to take part in the wrong thing at the wrong time.

Chapter 7

Cruel and Unusual

Excessive bail shall not be required, nor excessive fines imposed, nor cruel and unusual punishments inflicted.
—*Constitution of the United States, Bill of Rights, Eighth Amendment*

No matter how senseless or brutal a crime is, justice can only be served if legal procedures are followed and constitutional amendments regarding punishment are upheld. Anything else is vigilante "justice," which serves only to make a mockery of our legal system. In 1917, a mob of thousands took it upon themselves to dish out their own brand of justice to a man who was presumed guilty of a crime. In the end, his "sentence" was every bit as much of an atrocity as the crime itself.

On the morning of April 30, 1917, a white teenage girl named Antoinette Rappal was riding her bike to Treadwell School, which was then on the outskirts of Memphis. The girl never arrived at school that day, nor did she arrive back home that afternoon. A search was launched for Antoinette, but it was four days before she was found. On the morning of May 3, searchers discovered her ravaged body and severed head in the Wolf River bottoms.

Shortly after the discovery of the body, a deaf-mute man named Dewitt Ford, who worked in the area, came forward and indicated that he had witnessed the crime. Though he was unable to speak intelligibly, he used gestures and pictures to point the finger of guilt at two wood choppers who worked in the area. Though both had alibis for the time of Antoinette's death, one of them, a black man named Ell Person, ultimately admitted that he had seen the girl on the day she disappeared. This was not incriminating in and of itself, however, as Antoinette's daily route took her down Macon Road—the very road where Person worked. In fact, Person told authorities that he saw the girl nearly every morning as she rode to school. The police were suspicious of the wood chopper

Treadwell School. *Shelby County Archives.*

Wolf River. *Memphis and Shelby County Room, Memphis Public Library & Information Center.*

but had no real proof of his involvement so they decided to look for other evidence.

Forensic science at the time suggested that a person who was murdered would have the image of their murderer reflected in their eyes. Based on this theory, Antoinette's body was exhumed and her eyelids opened. Investigators claimed that they saw a shadowy figure of a man in the girl's eyes and that it matched the general appearance of Ell Person. Meanwhile, officers went to Person's home and searched through his belongings. They uncovered a pair of freshly washed pants and a pair of freshly scrubbed shoes. This, they seemed to think, indicated that Person was trying to wash evidence from his clothing.

The authorities believed that these things conclusively implicated Person in Antoinette's murder. He was soon brought down to the station and interrogated for many hours. Person denied any involvement in the crime. Seeing that their interrogation tactics were not working and growing frustrated, sheriff's deputies began to beat the man. After that was done, they pointed to Person's shoes and said, "There's blood on your shoes!" Of course, the blood belonged to Person, himself, and had come from the beating he had just sustained. Nonetheless, this last accusation proved too much for Person to handle and he finally confessed to the crime.

Remember at this point in the story that Ell Person was a man who was exhausted, beaten and intimidated. He found himself at the mercy of the police officers who not only did not believe him, but who were also actually cruel to him. Person had likely reached the end of his rope and hoped that if he simply confessed, it would all be over. Of course, this is a common scenario in cases of false confession. And while it was never proven that Person's confession was actually coerced, the circumstances surrounding it would seem to indicate as much.

Due to the public outcry for justice, Ell Person was soon transported to the Tennessee State Prison in Nashville for his own protection instead of being locked up in the local jail. Even there, it was learned that an angry mob from Memphis was heading to Nashville to get him, and Person was moved to a different facility. The mob was undeterred, however, and knew that eventually Person would be returned to Memphis. Fearing that adequate justice would not be carried out, mob members quietly waited for an opportunity to get hold of the man. When a court date for Person was finally set, the leaders of the mob knew it was only a matter of time. They began to stop every passenger train coming from the north or east into Memphis and searched for the "confessed" killer.

When officials heard of the mob's tactics, they put Person on a train to Alabama and then on another train that would carry him through Mississippi and into Memphis. Someone must have tipped off the mob, for although this train was coming from the south, the mob stopped the train several miles outside of Memphis. Approximately twenty-five men boarded the train and took Ell Person from the deputies who were guarding him. Amazingly, the deputies apparently did little to stop the vigilantes. It did seem that mob rule had taken over the sensibilities of everyone involved in the case, and perhaps the deputies were no exception. In fact, the following edition of the newspaper outlined when and where the lynching of Ell Person was to take place, yet no one did anything to try to prevent it from happening.

The lynching was scheduled to take place on May 22 at the Wolf River bridge, near the site of the murder. On the morning of the lynching, thousands of people had assembled at the bridge. Of these, many were children who were kept out of school for the day by their parents who wanted them to witness the lynching. The mob and the spectators were not the only ones who were there at the bridge that morning. Vendors selling everything from sandwiches to chewing gum were also present, and it was reported that their sales were quite high. It is unclear just how many people actually showed up for the lynching. Early estimates put the number at around three thousand, while later reports stated that as many as fifteen thousand were on hand to see the execution of Ell Person. In addition, there were estimated to be thousands more who arrived on the scene just a little too late to witness the lynching.

Shortly after the car carrying Person arrived, Antoinette's mother also arrived on the scene. She had a simple statement to make: "I want to thank all my friends who have worked so hard in my behalf. Let the Negro suffer as my little girl suffered, only ten times worse."

Person was soon dragged to a clearing off the side of the road where he was chained to an enormous log. It was then announced that he wished to make a statement. Somehow, even with thousands of people as witnesses— or maybe *because* there were thousands of people as witnesses—there are three different accounts regarding the statement that Ell Person made. The first of these accounts says that Person tried to speak, but could not be heard over the din of the crowd. Another story says that the accused once again confessed to the crime and admitted that he deserved the punishment he was about to receive. The third account seems most plausible. According to that story, just before the lynching began, the mob asked Person if anyone else had been involved in the killing of Antoinette Rappal. When Person hesitated, mob members began to prompt him, suggesting that Dewitt Ford, the deaf-mute, or Dan Armstrong, another black wood chopper, had been involved. Person finally conceded that both men had taken part in the rape and murder of the young girl.

There is no way to know with certainty what Person's motives were for naming the other two men as accomplices, but it seems likely that being faced with a torturous death, Person would have been willing to say anything to escape his fate. In spite of his cooperation with the mob, the lynching proceeded.

Person was doused with ten gallons of gasoline and was then lit on fire with a match. As the smoke began to billow up around him, he sucked in as much of the toxic air as he could, clearly in an effort to speed up his own death. Thankfully, his tactic seemed to work. Ell Person died quickly and never uttered a single scream, even as the flames attacked his body.

After Person's body had been burned to little more than bone and cartilage, his ears were cut off, followed by his head. Several members of the mob took the head and drove down to Beale Street, where they tossed it out of the car at the feet of several black men who were standing around chatting. The mob members said, "Take this with our compliments." The severed head was soon turned over to county authorities.

Active members of the mob—the very ones who had pulled Ell Person from the train—then proceeded to track down and abduct Dewitt Ford and Dan Armstrong. The unofficial word was that the two would be lynched the following day in the same manner as Person had been. Before long, however, several reputable citizens who lived in the area near the crime scene came forward and provided alibis for Ford and Armstrong. The mob immediately released the two men, but Ford, who had been so traumatized by the event, ran straight to the police station, hoping to be placed in a jail cell for his own protection. He was assured that he would not be harmed and was sent home. No one else was ever implicated in the crime.

The lynching of Ell Person was unusual by lynching "standards" in that it was done in broad daylight with no attempt to hide the identities of members of the mob. It was generally assumed that the mob would face no legal repercussions and that assumption proved to be true. Both the core of the mob—the twenty-five or so men who actively abducted and murdered Ell Person—and the thousands who looked on while a man was brutally killed all got away with murder on that May morning in Memphis.

One has to wonder if and how the story would have been different if Ell Person had been a white man. Obviously, the rape and murder of a sixteen-year-old girl would be enough to get any town riled up, but how much did race play a role in the situation? Would a white suspect have sat undisturbed in jail and awaited prosecution? Or would mob mentality have still come into play?

The likely answer is that the brutal nature of the crime itself sparked the initial outrage of the citizens of Memphis. From there it seems probable that racial prejudices of the time ultimately added fuel to the fire—both figuratively and literally. In the grand scheme of things, of course, the motive for vigilante justice is irrelevant. When the letter of the law is ignored, the results can be tragic.

Chapter 8

Mistaken Identity

The morning of August 10, 1921, started out like any other in the city of Memphis, with folks just trying to make it through another dog day of summer. By noon, however, the city was shaken to its core. Three people were dead and four were wounded in one of the most senseless tragedies in local history.

In 1921, 495 Union Avenue (the property now home to the Commercial Appeal) was a Ford Motor plant. August 10 was payday for the plant's employees, and the payroll routine was a mundane weekly occurrence. Because of the sizable sum of cash that the payroll required, it was customary for two police officers to escort Ford officials to the bank. On this particular morning, Ford employees Edgar McHenry and Howard Gamble drove a late model Ford to the police station on Adams to pick up the two officers who would accompany them to the Central State Bank. The two officers, Carraway and Harris, climbed into the car and the foursome reached Central State in just moments. Inside the bank, the payroll bag was filled with $8,500 cash—a process that took only five minutes. The four then got back into the car and drove to the Ford plant. A four-man escort for a bag of cash, particularly when two of those men were police officers, might sound overly cautious. As the story will soon reveal, however, one can never be too careful when dealing with money.

Upon the payroll car's arrival, a late model, dark blue Cadillac swooped in from behind and blocked the car from driving away. Four men wearing masks hopped out of the Cadillac and pointed their guns at the payroll car. The bandits ordered the occupants of the Ford to hold their hands up. Although no one resisted the order, the bandits almost immediately opened fire on the payroll car. Carraway and Gamble were both fatally wounded. Officer Harris was seriously wounded in the backseat of the Ford, but Edgar McHenry, the very man holding the payroll bag, had not yet been

An aerial view of the Ford Motor Company facility. *Memphis and Shelby County Room, Memphis Public Library & Information Center.*

hit. Somehow, with bullets raining down around him, he managed to run from the car to the entrance of the Ford building. He and another clerk took the money and ran into a safe, closing the door behind them. Realizing that their robbery attempt had gone awry, the four masked men got back into the blue Cadillac and sped away.

Meanwhile, the Memphis Police Department had been notified about the shootings and robbery attempt. Lieutenant Vincent "Luke" Lucarini, a first-generation American born to Italian immigrants, was on duty when the call came in. The thirty-five-year-old had been recently promoted and was ambitious and enthusiastic about his job. For this reason, he decided to go after the gunmen himself. Knowing that the department's police cars would have a difficult time keeping up with a new Cadillac, he flagged down a civilian outside and asked for the use of his car. The civilian, local grocery store owner Joe Robilio, happened to drive a late model, dark blue Cadillac—similar to the one driven by the bandits.

Robilio drove his newly deputized Cadillac with Lieutenant Lucarini, Officers Bonds and Rodgers and another civilian named Eddie Heckinger as his passengers. By this time, reports had come in that the getaway car had traveled east on Union, then north on Dunlap and then east on Poplar. This was the last that anyone had seen of it. So Robilio headed east on Poplar past White Station, where a group of armed men were assembled. These men, believing that the speeding Cadillac was being driven by the bandits, phoned the police in Collierville to let them know that the getaway car was headed that way. For reasons unknown, these men did not try to stop the car themselves and therefore gave no indication to the car's passengers of the mistaken identity. Lucarini, in fact, even said that he was certain the men had seen his uniform.

Collierville deputy Morris Irby and a posse of more than fifty other officers and civilians positioned themselves on the side of the road, waiting for the blue Cadillac to appear. Soon, Irby spotted the car. He stood in the middle of the road, fired one shot into the air and ordered the driver of the car to stop. Not realizing the mix-up, Lucarini urged Robilio to keep driving. When Robilio failed to stop, the rest of the posse began shooting at the car, striking it nearly one hundred times.

Robilio was shot immediately and lost control of the car. Officer Bonds, at this time uninjured, was able to steer it to safety. Lucarini in the front seat had been fatally shot, and Eddie Heckinger was seriously wounded. Officers Bonds and Rodgers both climbed from the car with their hands above their heads, and Bonds waved his police cap like a white flag. Still failing to understand that they were shooting at officers of the law and innocent civilians, the posse continued firing at them, hitting Bonds multiple times with buckshot. Rodgers, miraculously, emerged from the incident uninjured.

By day's end, the young and ambitious Lieutenant Vincent Lucarini was dead, leaving behind his wife, Annie, and their twelve-year-old son. Also dead were Officer Polk Carraway and Howard Gamble. Officer W.S. Harris and Eddie Heckinger were both seriously wounded, while Officer C.L. Bonds, Joe Robilio and Edgar McHenry sustained less critical injuries. The unscathed bandits were still on the loose.

Posses from at least a dozen counties in Tennessee, Arkansas and Mississippi spent the night searching for the murderous foursome, but no trace of them was found. Almost immediately, however, witnesses began coming forward and offering information. Some were able to identify a man who was driving a late model, dark blue Cadillac. Others had seen the same man loitering around the Ford Motor plant on previous paydays. The man witnesses had seen was Thomas Harriss, and he was promptly apprehended.

In spite of the fact that Harriss was identified by numerous witnesses, one witness seemed to pose the greatest threat to him and was singled out by cronies of Harriss. The witness, Charles Diffle, was visited at his home by two men, who threatened his life if he didn't leave town. Diffle remained steadfast and ultimately testified against Harriss at trial.

Harriss, of course, was just one of the bandits involved in the crime, but he seemed to be the ringleader of the foursome. He was known to be the driver of the stolen Cadillac and was even credited with formulating the initial plan behind the attempted heist. Upon apprehension, it was discovered that Harriss had sustained buckshot wounds in one of his shoulders.

After his arrest, police searched his home and found evidence that led them to two other suspects, brothers Orville and Jesse Jones. From there, the police tracked down the fourth and final suspect, Edwin Von Steinkirk, an interesting character of German descent who claimed to be a baron.

The dark blue Cadillac that was used in the attempted robbery was found hidden in Riverside Park on August 12. Its hiding place was not far from the home of Orville and Jesse Jones. Not surprisingly, the car turned out to be a stolen one and was later identified by its owner, a man named Malcolm Buckingham. It had been taken from him at gunpoint several days prior to the Ford payroll robbery attempt.

On September 20, 1921, the four gunmen went to trial. The evidence against them was overwhelming. Their fingerprints had been found in the stolen Cadillac. Guns and ammunition found in the home of Thomas Harriss matched the caliber of weapons and bullets used in the shooting. Though not physical in nature, the most compelling evidence presented by the prosecution was the testimony of more than 130 witnesses who had seen the gunmen either at the time of the crime or immediately before or after.

Thanks in part to the sheer number of witnesses involved, the trial dragged on for seven weeks. When the jury was finally charged, it deliberated for just shy of twenty-four hours before reaching a standstill. It wasn't that the defendants' guilt was in question, for all twelve jurors believed them to be guilty. Instead, they had reached an impasse on how to sentence them. Only seven of the jurors wanted to sentence them to death, a punishment that required unanimity. Finally, all of the jurors agreed to a sentence of life in prison.

The four convicted killers were then sent to the Tennessee State Penitentiary in Nashville, where they would presumably spend the rest of their lives. Just a few years into their sentences, however, the foursome managed to escape, though all were quickly apprehended. Somehow, in spite of their escapes, Thomas Harriss, Orville Jones, Jesse Jones and Edwin Von Steinkirk were pardoned and released less than fourteen years after they committed their violent crime. No further record of the four men could be found in the Memphis area, though by now they are almost certainly dead.

As for the others involved in the incident—those in the posse that fired the fatal shots at Lieutenant Lucarini and wounded three others—they were never charged with any crime. It was generally thought that they were acting in good faith, believing that they were shooting at a car full of murderers, not realizing that they were about to be guilty of the same offense.

Chapter 9

The Summer Avenue Slayer

In 1923, Berclair was a tiny town located just four miles east of Memphis. The area was sparsely dotted with homes, making it a bit more rural than suburban. Summer Avenue ran through the town and was, at the time, a dark and desolate road. So uninhabited was this road less travelled that one could commit murder there without fear of a witness or without anyone discovering the crime for hours. This is what happened on the night of January 27, when two people were executed right out in the open on Summer Avenue.

At about six o'clock the next morning, an unsuspecting milkman was headed into Memphis when he made a ghastly discovery. A car was parked on the side of the road with a young man dead behind its wheel. Just feet away from the car was another dead body, this one belonging to a young woman. The milkman quickly drove into town and notified the police. When the authorities arrived, it took very little probing to determine that the couple had been murdered. The young man's body bore three bullet wounds, while the woman's bore one. Supporting the fact that they had been shot was the discovery of four .25-caliber bullet casings nearby.

The identities of the two victims were soon established. The man was identified as Duncan Waller, a nineteen-year-old traveling salesman from Mayfield, Kentucky. The woman was Ruth McElwain Tucker, a twenty-year-old who lived near the present-day intersection of North Parkway and Cleveland Street with her mother. Upon speaking with their friends and relatives, it was determined that Waller had been carrying about $20 in cash at the time of the murder, while Tucker had been wearing approximately $200 worth of jewelry. When their bodies were discovered, all of the cash and jewelry were gone, leading the police to initially suspect robbery as a motive for the murders.

The authorities began investigating the backgrounds of the victims, hoping that some small clue might surface. They soon discovered that Ruth Tucker was actually married, though estranged from her husband. Just as in the Vadakin case, this prompted police to wonder why Ruth Tucker and Duncan Waller were travelling together late at night, and where exactly was Mr. Tucker?

Ellis Tucker, as it turned out, lived in Franklin, Tennessee, and had soon established an alibi for his whereabouts on the night of the murders. He was nowhere near Memphis. Further investigation also showed that there was no romantic involvement between Duncan Waller and Ruth Tucker. In fact, it was learned that Duncan was having a relationship with Ruth's friend, Peggy Wright, and there was even talk of a future marriage. With jealousy eliminated from the scenario and the solidity of his alibi, Mr. Tucker was soon cleared of any involvement in his wife's death and the death of her companion. Investigators then reverted back to the theory that robbery was the motive for the murders.

The detectives tried to piece together the events of the evening leading up to the murders. It seemed that Duncan, Ruth and Peggy had begun spending quite a bit of time together as a threesome. On the evening of the 27, Duncan and Ruth dropped off Peggy at the soda room where she worked, promising to come back later to visit her. From there, the two drove back to Ruth's mother's home, but didn't stay long. They told Mrs. McElwain that they would return later for Ruth's younger brother, William. At 8:00 p.m., the pair made good on their word and returned to the McElwain house, where they picked up William. The trio drove back to the soda room to visit with Peggy. While at the soda room, Duncan mixed up a few drinks of corn whiskey and soda water and both he and Ruth indulged in them. William chastised Ruth for drinking, but she seemed undeterred.

While at the soda room, it was decided that Ruth and Duncan would pick Peggy up at midnight and Peggy would spend the night at the McElwain home. It was also decided that in the meantime, Ruth and Duncan would pass the time by taking a drive. At about 10:00 p.m., the group left Peggy to finish her shift and William went his own way. Ruth and Duncan headed out into the night, and that was the last time anyone—other than the killer—saw them alive.

Once the evening's timeline had been established, investigators tried to find the gun that was used to kill the couple. They rounded up as many .25-caliber pistols as they could find and fired them to compare striking pin patterns. No match was found. There was no other evidence to be found, either. There were no unidentified fingerprints in the car and the rain had washed away any sign of footprints or other tracks. With little evidence and a motive as impersonal as robbery, the investigation came to a near standstill.

Four months later, however, the police got a break in the case when yet another murder occurred. On May 23, authorities were called to the scene of an attack on Summer Avenue near Highland. A young woman who had been shot in the neck had staggered to a nearby home, from which help was summoned. Her companion, a young man, was found shot to death in his car, which was parked by the side of the road. Again, as in the Duncan/Tucker murders, the back windshield had been shot out by .25-caliber bullets, suggesting that the killer fired the fatal shots from outside of the vehicle. And, once again, the motive appeared to be robbery. This time, however, he left a surviving witness.

The victim was soon identified as William Spencer, a twenty-four-year-old food store manager. His companion, who was shot but not killed, was determined to be a schoolteacher named Laura Wheaton Johnson.

In the first few days following the crime, it seemed likely that Laura would not recover from her wounds. In fact, early newspaper reports called the crime a "double murder." As time wore on, however, she began to show gradual signs of improvement and finally awoke. When detectives interviewed her, she relayed a story that the evidence had already told quite well. The young couple had pulled over to the side of the road so that William could light a cigarette. While stopped, gunshots suddenly came from behind them. Four bullets hit William and one hit Laura. Though seriously injured, Laura was able to leap from the car. At this point, the assailant grabbed her roughly and snatched her white gold watch from her wrist. Laura pulled away and ran to a nearby house, where she collapsed. Unfortunately, Laura had scarcely gotten a glance at the shooter.

With the revelation of the stolen watch combined with the fact that William was found with his pockets pulled out and empty, it was clear that robbery was once again the motive for the crime. The police were convinced that they were dealing with the same killer in both incidents. Finally, though, there was a glimmer of hope in the case. Investigators were able to track down the maker of the stolen watch and retrieved the timepiece's serial number. Armed with that information, they began canvassing area pawnshops, waiting for the watch to appear. Less than two months after the murder of William Spencer, the watch finally showed up at a Beale Street pawnshop.

The watch had been pawned for $5.50 by a woman named Luada Barr. Mrs. Barr was quickly interrogated and she maintained that her husband had given her the watch as a gift. When she was short on cash, she decided to pawn it. Not entirely convinced of her innocence, the police held Luada

The Shelby County Courthouse. *Memphis and Shelby County Room, Memphis Public Library & Information Center.*

in a cell until her husband, Charlie Barr, could be questioned. It took very little time for the authorities to pick up Charlie and bring him down to the station. When they did, he had nothing but denials to offer them, maintaining that he had never before seen the watch. After additional interrogation and a subsequent lockup in a cell, Charlie was ready to change his story. He then asserted that his wife's former boyfriend had given her the watch along with a .25-caliber pistol. His mention of the pistol was especially interesting as the policed had not yet said anything about a gun. But, wanting to make sure they had covered all of their bases, the police went out and found Luada's former boyfriend, George Tunstall. Mr. Tunstall was apparently shocked by the allegations presented to him and denied them all vehemently. He ultimately convinced the police of his innocence and was released.

Investigators decided then to search the Barr home in hopes of finding the murder weapon. Not only did they succeed, but they also found one of the diamond rings that had belonged to Ruth Tucker. This was more than enough evidence to charge Charlie with the murders.

Before the case could go to trial, Charlie's employer hired a team of renowned attorney's to represent him. These lawyers advised Charlie to answer no further questions without their approval. One day, however, the detectives in the case assembled in an effort to provoke Charlie to confess. Gathered in a room with the accused present, they began to discuss the details of the case and passed the evidence around. Barr eventually grew uncomfortable with this. He finally stood and, in front of the room full of police officers, confessed to shooting all four victims.

In February 1924, the case against Charlie Barr was brought to trial at the Shelby County Courthouse. The defendant's attorneys worked feverishly to make him a legally innocent man, but to no avail. After a thirteen-day trial, the jury returned with a guilty verdict and sentenced Charlie to death. On August 29, 1926, Charlie Barr was electrocuted at the Tennessee State Prison in Nashville.

Chapter 10

The Cigarette Girl

When Daisy Nowicki died at the age of ninety-three in the little town of Bethel Springs, Tennessee, she had lived a long and full life. She had three grandchildren and four great-grandchildren to her credit, she was a member of the Order of the Eastern Star and she belonged to Raleigh Christian Church. At the time of her death in 1998, she had outlived her only son by more than three years. She had also survived two husbands. What one might never have guessed, however, is that this seemingly respectable lady had shot her first husband to death in one of Memphis's most notorious murders some sixty-three years prior.

Daisy Alexander Roberts was a young woman employed at Goldsmith's in downtown Memphis when she met her future husband, Brenton Root. Brenton (more commonly known as Brit) was the son of an Episcopal minister from Chicago. Brit and Daisy were wed in 1927, and within five years they had a son, whom they named George. The two had also built a home near Kimball Avenue and Getwell Road. Despite their apparent marital bliss, Brit found faithfulness difficult and had already begun to stray. By 1934, the couple had separated for the first of several times to come. During these separations, Brit would date as many women as he could manage, even keeping a log of his dates. In 1935, Brit had become interested in a nineteen-year-old woman named Lucille Underwood, who worked selling cigarettes at the Hotel DeVoy. Lucille was a cute girl with a charming smile who played the part of pinup well. And though she was very much attracted to Brit, she wanted nothing to do with him once she learned he was married. Brit, though typically a ladies' man, seemed determined to be with Lucille. Perhaps it was the challenge of getting a woman who had rejected him; whatever the reason, Brit tried his best to win Lucille's affections, to no avail.

In November 1935, it seemed as though Brit had had a change of heart. He called Daisy on the phone and told her that he was through sowing his wild oats and that he only wanted to be with her. He invited her, along with four of their friends, to a dance being held at the Hotel DeVoy. It is at this point in the tale that we are forced to speculate. Brit would have known, of course, that Lucille would be working at the hotel that night. Yet he had just professed his love to his wife and had asked her for a fresh start. So what was his motive in taking Daisy to a dance in the very place that Lucille would be working? Could he have been attempting to make Lucille jealous by showing up with his wife?

Whatever his reasons, he, his wife and the two other couples went to the dance that evening. Things seemed to be going well and Brit and Daisy danced together while listening to the orchestra. After their dance, Daisy saw Lucille across the room and apparently recognized her as one of Brit's many women. Enraged, Daisy made her way across the room and dragged the cigarette girl to the table where Brit was sitting. Daisy then taunted her husband.

"Why don't you buy a pack of cigarettes?" she asked him.

Brit, who apparently found the scenario amusing, said to Lucille, "Okay, sweetheart, give me a pack of cigarettes."

This, of course, enraged Daisy further and she immediately slapped her husband in the face.

Still amused, Brit turned back to Lucille and said, "All right, honey, give me that pack of cigarettes."

No sooner had the words escaped his lips, Daisy slapped him again.

Brit just smiled and said, "You can keep me from buying a pack of cigarettes from her, but you can't keep me from loving her."[8]

These words were simply too much for Daisy to bear and she immediately ran from the room. Her friends went after her and finally took her home. At home, she mulled over the events of the evening, growing more furious with each passing hour. When she had finally had enough, she grabbed her keys and her handgun and drove to Brit's house—the very house that the couple had once shared.

At 1:45 a.m. on November 3, 1935, Daisy walked into Brit's bedroom and woke him up. "Look at me, darling," she said and promptly shot him five times.

Daisy then picked up the phone and told the operator that she had shot her husband. An ambulance was quickly dispatched, but paramedics were unable to help Brenton Root. He died on the way to the hospital. On Brit's death certificate, the cause and manner of death were spelled out clearly: "This man was shot four times in torso and once in wrist by his wife while in a high nervous tension."

The former DeVoy Hotel. *Memphis and Shelby County Room, Memphis Public Library & Information Center.*

Lucille Underwood. *Special Collections, University of Memphis Libraries.*

Daisy was soon arrested and charged with first-degree murder. Nevertheless, she was permitted to attend her husband's funeral on November 6. While there, she was reported to have cried hysterically beside Brit's coffin. After the service, Brit's father, Reverend Benjamin Root, publicly declared his support for Daisy. Just two weeks later, while Brit's

Daisy Root. *Special Collections, University of Memphis Libraries.*

mother was visiting Daisy in jail, the reverend was delivering a sermon on forgiveness at his church in Chicago. Speaking of Daisy, he had this to say:

> *There is no merit in the fact that I forgive this girl. How could a Christian do otherwise? Forgiveness is as natural as the sunrise, or the smile of a*

little child. My heart still bleeds. She will always be my dear, little girl. Somehow, in some way, this must work out for the ultimate good.[9]

After her indictment, Daisy was released on bond and stayed with her parents. They were taking care of little George, who was four years old at the time of the murder. Daisy's trial began on January 24, 1936. Her lawyers decided to use a battered-woman-syndrome defense, alleging that Brit often beat his wife and once even caused her to have a miscarriage by beating her so severely. If that wasn't enough, her attorney's also painted a vivid picture of the womanizing side of Brenton Root. When they were finished, Brit looked like a scoundrel.

But the prosecutor was quick to point out that, womanizer or not, Brit did not deserve to die. He also set out to paint an equally damaging picture of Daisy, forcing her to admit that the two had engaged in sex before marriage, that she was also guilty of having had an affair and that she had once attempted suicide. By the end of the trial, the reputations of both Daisy and Brenton had been badly tarnished.

On January 30, the attorneys gave their closing arguments. On January 31, the jury returned with a verdict. The twelve men had found Daisy Root guilty of second-degree murder. The judge sentenced her to ten years in the state penitentiary. Daisy did not report to prison right away, as she was allowed to remain free on bond while her lawyers appealed her conviction. The Tennessee Supreme Court opted not to overturn her conviction, but instead reduced her charge to voluntary manslaughter and her sentence to two years. The Supreme Court judges apparently had sympathy for Daisy, stating that Brit had been "lecherous in the extreme."

Daisy Root had served fourteen months of this two-year sentence when Tennessee Governor Gordon Browning pardoned her. She returned to her parents' home to resume the rearing of her son. She told reporters that she was dedicating her full time and attention to George, who by then was six years old. She went on to say that she hoped people would eventually forget the whole situation and that she would be able to live a normal life.

It seems that Daisy's wish was fulfilled. Newspapers soon quit reporting on her and she eventually left Memphis and began a new life in Bethel Springs. She then became Daisy Nowicki—homemaker, wife, mother and eventually grandmother and great-grandmother. Though it is nearly certain that the people closest to Daisy knew about her past, it seems that she was able to slip into the oblivion for which she had longed so many years ago.

Chapter 11

Memphis's Merry Widow

Many law enforcement officials maintain that one of the worst aspects of their jobs is notifying the next of kin after a death. When police officers came across the body of Ed Gill in the early morning hours of January 3, 1949, however, at least one deputy found the situation comical. "Heh, heh, heh," a deputy sheriff was quoted as saying. "Alma's gone and shot herself another husband!"[10]

Mrs. Alma Herrin Cook Cox Calvert McClavy Theede Gill, you see, was now widowed for the fourth time.

Alma Herrin was born on the seedier side of town in 1895. Her parents were poverty-stricken, and at age sixteen, Alma began doing the only thing she knew to bring in a little extra money for the family. She became a prostitute, frequently working on Vance Avenue and charging one to two dollars per "customer." This earned her the nickname of "Vance Avenue Alma."

At seventeen, Alma tried to leave that life behind. She met a man named Halpin Cox and the two of them ran off to Arkansas to elope. The honeymoon was very short-lived, however, and Alma had filed for divorce and moved back home with her newly widowed mother before her eighteenth birthday.

By the time she was nineteen, Alma had married again, this time to a Little Rock railroad worker named Roy Calvert. The marriage was a rocky one from the beginning, and Roy was reported to be a heavy drinker. In 1919, Alma committed murder for the first time when she shot her husband dead. Due to the violent nature of their marriage, Alma was found not guilty by reason of justifiable homicide. Again, she returned home to live with her mother. She also returned to her former occupation, and Vance Avenue Alma was working the streets again.

One night, Alma picked up an unexpected customer. It was her first husband, Halpin Cox. Soon the two had remarried. The couple had been married for a few uneventful years when Halpin was killed in a traffic accident in Arkansas. Alma was now a widow for the second time, though she played no role in Cox's death. With no other "skills," Alma once more resorted to her old life as a prostitute. This time, however, Alma found the streets to be a rough place to work and she began working in a brothel. For years she was successful as a "housegirl," but eventually years of living a hard life caught up with her and her looks began to suffer. Finally, the brothel's madam told Alma that her "career" there was over. Alma moved to another brothel, this one of lower class than the first.

It was while working at this second brothel that Alma met her fourth husband, Mike McClavey. McClavey was old enough to be Alma's father but was by all accounts a sweet man with a good heart. He wanted to rescue Alma from her life of prostitution, and as her husband, he provided for her every need. The newlyweds moved into Mike's house on Avery Street and Mike even gave his new wife a gambling allowance, as this was her one remaining vice. In time, though, Alma wanted more money for gambling than Mike was willing to spend. To bring in additional income, Alma suggested renting a room to a boarder. Mike agreed, even though he seemed to understand where this newfound money would be spent. Soon, they had found their first boarder, a man closer in age to Alma named C.E. Miller.

It wasn't long before Alma and Miller were having an affair. Mike, who was not a stupid man, warned his wife to leave Miller alone. His wife, however, decided it would be better to do away with Mike than to end her affair with Miller. On December 20, 1927, Michael McClavey was found shot to death in his bedroom. At the time of the shooting, Alma was in another room in the house. She told police that she suddenly heard gunshots and ran into the room to find Mike dead. When the authorities asked Alma where Miller was, she simply said, "He seems to have vanished."

The investigators on the case soon learned about the death of Roy Calvert in Arkansas and began looking anew at the McClaveys' marriage. They uncovered witnesses who would testify that Alma had been having an affair with Miller. They also heard from Miller's associates that he had vowed to kill Mike should he ever interfere with his and Alma's relationship. The final bit of incriminating evidence came when they learned that, shortly before Mike's death, Alma had given Miller a gun as a gift. The investigators had established motive and found sufficient evidence, and they were keeping tabs on one of their suspects. Now they just had to locate their second suspect. They began following Alma in the hopes that she would lead them to Miller. Soon, their hopes were realized and the two suspected killers were in custody.

In the spring of 1928, the pair went to trial. Miller was convicted of second-degree murder and sentenced to fifteen years in the Tennessee State Prison. Alma was convicted of being an accessory after the fact and was sentenced to ten years in the same facility.

Having no trouble meeting men anywhere she went, it was in the Tennessee State Prison that Alma met her future fifth husband, William "Bill" Theede. Theede was also serving time for murder, but he estimated that both he and Alma would be released at about the same time if given time off for good behavior. His estimate proved to be quite close. Alma was released from prison after doing less than half of her sentence, and Bill was released just a few months later. The two were married in Hernando, Mississippi, just south of Memphis in 1933.

Bill and Alma, along with Alma's mother, soon moved to a tiny house just outside of town at 3077 Ford Road. They made their living by raising pigs and chickens, but theirs was not a peaceful existence. It was only a matter of time before Alma had threatened the life of her fifth husband. At that, Bill Theede filed for divorce and it was soon granted. Once again, Alma and her mother were living alone together. They spent the next several years in poverty, struggling to keep ownership of the shack in which they lived.

Eventually, Alma met Ed Gill, who would become her sixth husband. Her track record with men was, by then, a dismal one. Two divorces and three deaths must have surely seemed strange to Ed, but as is often the case, love can be blind. Ed and Alma were married in 1946, and Ed moved into the Ford Road house with Alma and her mother. The Gills had soon settled into life as a couple and there were no reports of trouble between them. As far as anyone knew, they were blissfully married. All of that changed, however, when Ed was found dead from a gunshot wound on that early rainy morning in 1949.

When the police showed up at the Gill home after discovering Ed's body, Alma feigned surprise. She maintained that Ed had been on a drinking binge for weeks, suggesting that his inebriated state might have contributed to his death. Her mother verified the story, but the investigators were undeterred. Soon they had confiscated Alma's gun, a .38-caliber pistol, and ballistics tests matched it to the bullet that had killed Ed Gill. Faced with this evidence, Alma had little choice but to confess to the crime and put the best spin on it that she possibly could. She maintained that she and Ed had been arguing and that he had pulled the gun. She said that they struggled for it and it accidentally went off, striking Ed.

On January 19, Alma Gill faced arraignment for the murder of her husband and she pled not guilty. In the beginning, Mrs. Gill seemed quite confident that she would be acquitted, maintaining that as long as the jurors

16	DEPARTMENT OF PUBLIC HEALTH **CERTIFICATE OF DEATH** DIVISION OF VITAL STATISTICS			

THIS BECOMES A LEGAL RECORD WHEN PROPERLY EXECUTED AND WILL BE PLACED IN PERMANENT FILE.

WRITE PLAINLY WITH PERMANENT INK OR TYPEWRITER.

PHYSICIAN LAST IN ATTENDANCE MUST STATE CAUSE OF DEATH AND SIGN MEDICAL CERTIFICATION. IF NO PHYSICIAN IN ATTENDANCE, HEALTH OFFICER (OR CORONER, IF INQUEST WAS HELD) MUST COMPLETE AND SIGN MEDICAL CERTIFICATION. POWER OF SIGNATURE CANNOT BE DELEGATED.

CAUSE OF DEATH. ENTER ONLY ONE CAUSE PER LINE FOR A, B, C. * THIS DOES NOT MEAN CAUSE OF DYING SUCH AS HEART FAILURE, ASTHENIA, ETC. IT MEANS THE DISEASE, INJURY OR COMPLICATION WHICH CAUSED DEATH.

FUNERAL DIRECTOR OR PERSON DISPOSING OF BODY, MUST FILE CERTIFICATE WITH LOCAL REGISTRAR WITHIN 72 HOURS AFTER DEATH AND PRIOR TO TRANSPORTATION BY COMMON CARRIER OR REMOVAL FROM STATE.

ALL ITEMS ARE TO BE COMPLETE AND ACCURATE.

FORM 120

STATE OF TENNESSEE
COOPERATING WITH NATIONAL OFFICE OF VITAL STATISTICS

BIRTH NO.   DEATH NO.

1. NAME Edward Clay Gill   2. DATE OF DEATH Jan. 2, 1949

3. COLOR OR RACE W   4. SEX Male   5. SINGLE, MARRIED, WIDOWED OR DIVORCED Married   6. DATE OF BIRTH 11-26-1883   7. AGE (IN YEARS LAST BIRTHDAY) 65   IF UNDER 1 YR. MONTHS 1 DAYS 6   IF UNDER 24 HRS. HOURS MINS.

8. PLACE OF DEATH Suddenly on Ford Road
A. COUNTY Shelby   B. CIVIL DISTRICT
C. CITY OR TOWN Memphis, rural   D. LENGTH OF STAY IN THIS PLACE 27yrs.

9. USUAL RESIDENCE OF DECEASED
A. STATE Tenn.   B. COUNTY Shelby   C. CIVIL DISTRICT
D. CITY OR TOWN Memphis

E. NAME OF HOSPITAL OR INSTITUTION Peebles Road
E. STREET ADDRESS 3077 Ford Road

10A. USUAL OCCUPATION Laborer   10B. KIND OF BUSINESS OR INDUSTRY Hauling   11. SOCIAL SECURITY NUMBER

12. WAS DECEASED EVER IN U.S. ARMED FORCES? no   13. BIRTHPLACE Tennessee   14. CITIZEN OF WHAT COUNTRY?

15. FATHER'S NAME Unknown   16. MOTHER'S MAIDEN NAME Unknown   17. INFORMANT Mrs. Ed Gill, 3077 Ford Road

MEDICAL CERTIFICATION

18. CAUSE OF DEATH
1 DISEASE OR CONDITION DIRECTLY LEADING TO DEATH* (A) This man was found shot in Peoples Road. Pistol
ANTECEDENT CAUSES
MORBID CONDITIONS, IF ANY, GIVING RISE TO ABOVE CAUSE (A) STATING THE UNDERLYING CAUSE LAST. DUE TO (B) bullet in back of head - Homicide
DUE TO (C)
2. OTHER SIGNIFICANT CONDITIONS

19A. DATE OF OPERATION   19B. MAJOR FINDINGS OF OPERATION   20A. AUTOPSY YES NO   20B. FINDINGS AT AUTOPSY

21A. ACCIDENT SUICIDE HOMICIDE Homicide   21B. PLACE OF INJURY Shelby Co. Highway   21C. PLACE OF INJURY Peebles Road RURAL COUNTY Shelby STATE Tenn.
21D. TIME OF INJURY Jan. 2 1949   21E. INJURY OCCURRED NOT WHILE AT WORK   21F. HOW DID INJURY OCCUR? Shot with pistol

22. I HEREBY CERTIFY THAT THE DECEASED DIED ON THE DATE AND FROM THE CAUSE STATED ABOVE
SIGNATURE C. W. Miller, Coroner   ADDRESS 391 Gaston   DATE 1-14-49

23A. BURIAL, CREMATION, REMOVAL Removal   23B. DATE OF BURIAL 1-4-49   23C. NAME OF Cemetery or Crematory Obion   23D. LOCATION Obion, Tennessee

24. FUNERAL DIRECTOR National Funeral Home, 1177 Union   25. REGISTRATION DIST. NO.   26. DATE SIGNED BY LOCAL REG. 1-17-49   27. REGISTRAR'S SIGNATURE

Ed Gill's death certificate. *Shelby County Archives.*

did not take her past into consideration, she would most certainly be found innocent. She also seemed more concerned about her mother's well-being than of her own, stating once that, "If anything happens to me, it will be the end of my mother."[11]

But Alma's mother, Mrs. Nettie Herring, was optimistic. "If the truth is put before the jurors," she said, "my baby will come home."

At the trial, things weren't looking so good for Alma. Perhaps fearing a first-degree murder conviction, she pled guilty on the last day of the trial to murder in the second degree. She was sentenced to a maximum term of ten years in the state penitentiary.

Alma apparently carried no ill feelings toward the judge or prosecutor, for in December she sent Christmas gifts to the two men who had sealed her fate. To Judge Robert Krinkle, the merry widow sent a green, handmade, crocheted doily set. To District Attorney John Heiskell, she sent a similar doily set in lavender.

In 1955, Alma was paroled and released from prison. It was not long after her release that Alma married for the seventh and final time. Little is known

The former Tennessee State Penitentiary in Nashville. *Library of Congress.*

about that marriage, only that it was relatively short-lived and ultimately ended in divorce. Swearing off marriage then, Alma began using the last name of Theede once more. In 1970, Alma Theede, better known for most of her life as Vance Avenue Alma, died at Baptist Hospital in Memphis at the age of seventy-five.

Chapter 12

The Assassination of a Dreamer

Racial tensions have always run high in Memphis—even into the twenty-first century. But in all of Memphis history, perhaps the era that saw the most racial turmoil was the late 1960s. Desegregation of the public schools was well underway, and this was something to which many whites were vehemently opposed. Many black citizens of the city were becoming more outspoken in their demand for equality, staging sit-ins, boycotts and other tactics to bring about change. If these things were not enough, consider that the mayor of Memphis at the time, Henry Loeb, was a known segregationist. With these factors in mind, it is no wonder that racial tensions were bubbling and would soon boil over.

The beginning of the end came in February 1968, when thirteen hundred black sanitation workers went on strike. The goal of the strike was to secure equal treatment and equal pay, regardless of the worker's race. Before the strike, the average black sanitation worker's salary was $1.70 per hour, an amount just slightly higher than minimum wage. This was so low that as many as 40 percent of them qualified for welfare assistance. Black workers were also typically sent home without pay when the weather was bad, while the white workers were allowed to finish their shifts. Among the final straws that led to the strike were the deaths of two black sanitation workers, Echol Cole and Robert Walker, who had been forced to use old and faulty garbage-collecting equipment. The two got caught in the rear of the garbage truck and were compacted like trash, killing them instantly.

The strike had been ongoing for several weeks when Dr. Martin Luther King Jr. was asked to come to Memphis to help. He first arrived in Memphis on March 18 to speak at a rally. He assured his followers that he would return to lead the sanitation strike march that was scheduled for the end of the month. On March 28, King returned to Memphis and led the group of mostly peaceful demonstrators through the city streets. Dr. King always advocated peaceful protests, teaching and preaching that there was nothing to be gained through violence. Unfortunately for everyone involved in the march, however, there were a few demonstrators who decided to start some trouble. These young people ripped the wooden handles from their protest signs and used them to break out store windows. After this turn of events, looting soon began and pandemonium quickly ensued. As a result of the chaos, dozens of people were injured and one person was killed. Martin Luther King was quickly led from the scene to safety.

King vowed to return to Memphis in April to lead another march. However, the city of Memphis blamed the violence from the March 28 demonstration on him, and officials secured an injunction to stop the April march from taking place. King and his attorneys worked to have the injunction overturned, but King maintained that the march would take place—with or without an injunction. On April 3, the civil rights leader returned to Memphis with every intention of proceeding with the upcoming demonstration. On the night of his return to the city, he delivered his famous "I've Been to the Mountaintop" speech at the Mason Temple in southwest Memphis. Though always at ease in front of a crowd, King seemed especially at peace that evening, even as he made references to threats that had been made upon his life:

> *And then I got to Memphis. And some began to say the threats, or talk about the threats that were out. What would happen to me from some of our sick white brothers? Well, I don't know what will happen now. We've got some difficult days ahead. But it doesn't matter with me now. Because I've been to the mountaintop. And I don't mind. Like anybody, I would like to live a long life. Longevity has its place. But I'm not concerned about that now. I just want to do God's will.*

The next day, Dr. King and his attorneys spent a great deal of time in court challenging the constitutionality of the injunction. King maintained, "We stand on the First Amendment. In the past on the basis of conscience we have had to break injunctions and if necessary we may do it."[12] The business day ended with no clear resolution to the matter of the injunction. That evening, Dr. King was looking forward to having dinner at the home of Reverend and Mrs. Billy Kyles. From there, he would be attending a meeting.

At around 6:00 p.m., King stepped out onto the balcony of the Lorraine Motel. In the parking lot below stood the Reverend Jesse Jackson and musician Ben Branch. King leaned over the balcony and said to Branch, "Ben, make sure you play 'Take My Hand, Precious Lord' in the meeting tonight. Play it real pretty."[13] The trio chatted for another minute and then King straightened up and turned to go back into his room. It was at that moment that a shot rang out from across the parking lot and a bullet hit Dr. King in his right cheek, shattering his jaw and then traveling down his spine. Police and paramedics arrived on the scene in minutes, and the victim was transferred to St. Joseph's Hospital. At 7:05 p.m., thirty-nine-year-old Dr. Martin Luther King Jr. was pronounced dead. He left behind his wife, Coretta Scott King, and his four children, Yolanda Denise King, Martin Luther King III, Dexter Scott King and Bernice Albertine King.

When the first police officers arrived on the scene, members of King's staff pointed out the back of the boardinghouse from which the shot apparently came. One patrolman ran toward the boardinghouse, where he met up with another officer. The two found fresh footprints in the mud in an alley alongside the building. One officer stayed to guard the prints, while the other officer continued down the block in search of the assassin. At the shop next door to the boardinghouse, the officer made a startling discovery. A green blanket was lying in the doorway of the shop. Upon inspection, it revealed a suitcase and a .30-06 hunting rifle equipped with a scope. The owner of the shop said that a white man running by had dropped the blanket and had then sped away in a white Ford Mustang.

When investigators were unable to find any trace of the Mustang, they turned their attention back to the boardinghouse from which the fatal shot

The .30-06 hunting rifle used to assassinate Dr. King. *Shelby County Archives.*

appeared to have been fired. The owner of the house, Bessie Brewer, told the detectives that a Mr. John Willard had taken a room in her house on the afternoon of April 4. Willard was originally assigned to Room 8, but after inspecting the room, he requested a change. He was then given room 5B, which gave him a clear view of the Lorraine Motel. Another of the house's tenants told police that Willard went back and forth to the shared bathroom several times. When the tenant heard the gunshot, he looked out of his door and saw Willard running toward the stairs.

Within hours of the shooting, angry rioters poured into the streets and smashed store windows, set buildings on fire and began looting. At least thirty people were injured and eighty people arrested in conjunction with the rioting, and four thousand National Guardsmen were sent to Memphis to maintain order. A 7:00 p.m., curfew was also enacted. Such incidents were not isolated to Memphis, however. Riots had broken out in other major cities, including Chicago and Washington, D.C.

Several days after the shooting, an abandoned white Mustang was discovered in Atlanta. The vehicle was registered to an Eric Galt. Department of Motor Vehicles records showed that Galt and Willard had almost identical physical descriptions. When the FBI ran fingerprints found on Galt's possessions and fingerprints found on the rifle, both came back as a match to James Earl Ray, an escaped convict.

Authorities questioned acquaintances of Ray with little success. His family said that they had not heard from him, and his former cellmates claimed to know little of his plans. One cellmate, however, did mention that Ray had talked about how easy it was to obtain a Canadian passport. It was not much to go on, but it was all investigators had.

On June 1, after going through nearly 200,000 passport applications, the Royal Canadian Mounted Police contacted the FBI because they had found a possible match. A passport photo of a George Ramon Sneyd bore a remarkable resemblance to James Earl Ray. Interestingly enough, the passport had been issued on April 24, less than three weeks after the assassination. Using the passport, Sneyd flew from Toronto to London on May 6. British authorities then joined in the hunt for Sneyd. On June 8, they had their man. James Earl Ray was arrested while trying to board a flight for Brussels.

Ray was soon extradited to Memphis, where he was placed under twenty-four-hour watch in a special cell. Authorities did not want to take a chance on James Earl Ray escaping from prison again, nor did they want him killed by angry prisoners before he went to trial. From his cell, Ray hired and fired one attorney before finally settling on Texas lawyer Percy Foreman. Ray told his attorney that he had not shot Martin Luther King, but admitted that he had purchased the murder weapon for a man named Raoul. Although

James Earl Ray. *Shelby County Archives.*

there was some evidence that Raoul existed and that the two men worked together on some petty crimes, nothing suggested that Raoul had been involved in the King assassination.

Whether Foreman actually believed the Raoul story is uncertain. He did not, however, think that he could make a jury believe it, in spite of an impressive record of acquittals to his credit. He explained to Ray that going to trial would mean the possibility of a death sentence and urged him to plead guilty. His client finally agreed.

On March 10, 1969, Ray appeared in court to enter his plea. While he admitted to shooting King, he also claimed that his role in the murder was part of a larger conspiracy. In exchange for his plea, James Earl Ray was sentenced to ninety-nine years in prison. On March 13, however, Ray wrote a letter to the judge who had heard his plea:

> *I wish to inform the Honorable Court that famous Houston attorney Percy Fourflusher* [sic] *is no longer representing me in any capacity. My reason for writing this letter is that I intend to file for a post conviction hearing.*[14]

James Earl Ray was recanting his confession and trying to revoke his guilty plea. He claimed that he had been coerced by Percy Foreman, suggesting that the lawyer did not want to blemish his record by having a client sentenced to death. He maintained that he had nothing to do with the King assassination at all. Although he took his case all the way to the Supreme Court, Ray was never granted a new trial.

While some might suppose that this would have been the end of the matter, such was not the case in this most controversial and notorious of crimes. Almost from the very beginning, there have been suspicions of a conspiracy in the King assassination. There were multiple reasons for this way of thinking. First of all, Dr. King was causing quite a stir across the nation and some wondered if the government simply wanted to be rid of him. Next, James Earl Ray hardly seemed sophisticated enough to pull off such an elaborate murder and subsequent escape on his own. Finally, one man came forward and admitted involvement in the King assassination conspiracy.

The man's name was Lloyd Jowers, and he was a former restaurant owner from Memphis. Jowers claimed that he was offered $100,000 by members of the mob to plan and execute King's assassination. The Shelby County attorney general opened an investigation to check out Jowers's claims. They found nothing to substantiate them and, in fact, learned that Jowers had paid others to back his story, as he believed his claims would land him a movie deal. In spite of this evidence that Jowers had made up the entire story, the King family believed him. They had believed from the beginning that, at the most, James Earl Ray had not acted alone, but was part of a greater conspiracy. They filed a wrongful death lawsuit for $100 against Jowers and won.

As it turned out, the King family even believed it was possible that James Earl Ray had nothing to do with King's death at all. In March 1997, Dexter King, one of Martin Luther King's sons who was seven years old at the time of the assassination, paid a surprise visit to James Earl Ray in prison. The two men sat down to talk, and Dexter finally asked Ray if he had murdered his father. Ray reportedly looked him straight in the eye and denied any involvement. Dexter told the convicted killer that he and his family believed him and would do everything they could to help him get a new trial. Despite their best efforts, there would never be a new trial.

Today, conspiracy theories still abound regarding the assassination of Dr. Martin Luther King Jr., and the whole truth may never be known. Could his murder have been the end result of a government plot aimed at silencing the civil rights leader and all he stood for? Could it have been the result of a mob conspiracy? Decades after the crime, it is unlikely that anyone will come forward and implicate themselves. The one and only person who truly had nothing else to lose—James Earl Ray—died in 1998 as an inmate at Brushy Mountain Correctional Complex in Petros, Tennessee. He was seventy years old.

Officially, of course, justice was served in the case. While some people may doubt Ray's guilt or believe that others out there were involved, it is surely more important to stay focused on King's life rather than on his senseless death at the hands of a coward. After all, his work, his struggles and his triumphs helped to lead our society to where it is today.

Chapter 13

Serial Killer of '69

In August 1969, the entire nation was reeling from the Tate/LaBianca murders in Los Angeles, California. It would be three months before Charles Manson and his "family" were arrested for the crime and no one knew who was responsible for the grisly deaths. No one knew when or where the next murder would occur. By the month's end, however, some folks would begin to suspect that the killer had come to Memphis.

The terror began on August 14. It was Tanya Dumas' birthday, and her parents were hosting a simple celebratory dinner in honor of the occasion. Tanya, her new husband, Mike, and her in-laws were expected to attend. The in-laws, middle-aged Roy and Bernalyn Dumas, never arrived, however. As the evening wore on with no word from the couple, their son began to grow concerned. He tried to call them at their home several times, but never received an answer. Eventually, he decided to go to their apartment at 1133 South Cooper Street and check on them.

When Michael Dumas arrived at his parents' apartment, he certainly could not have been prepared for the grisly scene awaiting him. He entered the home cautiously and called out to his parents, but received no response. Making his way through the apartment, he found his mother in her bed. She was nude, bound spread-eagle, gagged and dead. It appeared that she had been strangled to death. Upon making this discovery, Michael, who was by then in hysterics, called the police. He was unable to make himself search the rest of the apartment for fear of what he might find.

When the first officers arrived, they took a cursory look around the apartment. It was then that the body of Roy Dumas was found. He was bound and gagged in another room and also appeared to have been strangled, though there was a fair amount of blood on one side of his head. There was less blood on Bernalyn Dumas, though postmortem examinations revealed that she had been vaginally and anally penetrated by a pair of scissors, most likely after her death.

The bulk of the physical evidence in the Dumas case proved to be of very little help to the investigation. The stockings used to bind the victims, the scissors used to mutilate Mrs. Dumas and handkerchiefs apparently used by the killer had all come from the Dumases' home. A canvas of the neighborhood revealed very few clues and the Dumases had no known enemies. The only possible motive that investigators could come up with for the killings was robbery. Roy Dumas ran a business out of his home and police speculated that a robber might have assumed he would have large quantities of money in the apartment. Beyond that, the police had very little to go on. After the first few days, public interest in the case began to wane.

Eleven days later, the killer struck again. The victim this time was eighty-year-old Leila Jackson, a widow who ran a boardinghouse in the medical center district of town. After numerous phone calls to Mrs. Jackson went unanswered, her daughter-in-law sent her own son to check on the elderly woman. When the eighteen-year-old arrived, he found the house unlocked. This, of course, was unusual, so he went inside to investigate. He then discovered his grandmother's body and immediately called the police.

When police arrived on the scene, they were startled to immediately see the similarities between this scene and the scene of the Dumas murders. Leila Jackson, though not bound, was in the same spread-eagle position as Bernalyn Dumas. A nylon stocking was tied tightly around her neck and a butcher knife with a small amount of blood on it was lying between her legs. The implication was clear, but the autopsy report showed conclusively that the butcher knife had been used to vaginally penetrate Leila Jackson after her death.

Again, evidence was collected, but nothing of any significance was found that could help the police identify the killer. All of Mrs. Jackson's boarders were interrogated and checked out, but investigators were quickly able to clear them. Fingerprints found in Mrs. Jackson's home were compared to those found in the Dumas home, but none matched. The only possible link between the victims was that Leila Jackson also made her living from her home by renting out rooms. The killer might have suspected that she, too, would have had a stash of money somewhere. But could such depraved killings really be the result of a simple robbery?

After the discovery of Leila Jackson's body, news of the murders buzzed around town and people began to have concerns that a serial killer was on the loose. Citizens were urged by the police to keep their house and car doors locked. Sales of large dogs and guns increased substantially. The police department was flooded with calls from fearful citizens who reported suspicious persons all around. What started as panic, however, would turn into near hysteria just four days later when the next body was found.

Glenda Sue Harden was a twenty-one-year-old office worker at a downtown insurance company. A graduate of Kingsbury High School, she had recently become engaged to be married. On August 29, Glenda Sue received a paycheck for two weeks' work and planned to do a little shopping after work before meeting her fiancé. She was last seen alive while heading for her car in the parking lot. When she did not arrive home in time for her date with her fiancé, her frightened parents called the police. Knowing that a killer was out there, they already feared the worst.

Just before dawn the next morning, Glenda Sue's Mustang was found parked along the cobblestones by the Mississippi River. After this discovery, there was a renewed sense of urgency in the hunt for Glenda Sue. Many people, including her parents, began to resign themselves to the fact that something terrible had happened to the young woman. All day, searchers combed the area near where her car was found. Late that afternoon, two police officers came upon the body of the missing woman deep in the woods of Riverside Park. Her body was covered in stab wounds—fourteen to be exact. As with the other cases, very little physical evidence was found. Again, robbery seemed to be the only clear motive as there was no cash in the car or in Glenda Sue's possession, in spite of the fact that she had just been paid.

After the discovery of Glenda Sue's body, the police felt that it was time to confront the killer and face the public. Investigators gave an unexpected press conference in which they admitted that they believed all four murders had been committed by the same individual, though they were careful to not divulge too many details. Also during the press conference, they urged citizens to be careful and to be aware of their surroundings at all times. Very little urging was needed, however, as many people throughout the city—particularly women—were terrified. They had good reason to be.

Twelve days after Glenda Sue's body was discovered, the perpetrator killed his fifth and final victim. On the afternoon of September 11, screams were heard coming from an apartment on North Bellevue. Henry Currie, the building's custodian, was outside when the screaming began. The screams turned into a woman's desperate pleas of "Don't kill me! Don't kill me!" Henry ran toward the building and tried to determine from which apartment the screams had come. Just then, he heard someone running down the stairs.

The footsteps belonged to Wayne Armstrong, one of the building's tenants who also heard the screams. He peered out of his front door and spotted a man holding a bloody knife outside of another apartment. Wayne

Riverside Park, where the body of Glenda
Sue Harden was discovered. *Special Collections,
University of Memphis Libraries.*

slammed the door, grabbed his handgun and flung open the door once more, but the man with the knife was gone. Wayne, understanding that he might have just come face to face with the serial killer, dashed down the stairs and ran into Henry.

Before Wayne and Henry even had time to compare notes or formulate a plan, the man with the knife ran out from behind the building and headed for the street. Wayne shouted at him to stop and he actually paused for a moment. Then, thinking better of it, he took off down the street. Wayne and Henry immediately gave chase. Wayne fired three shots, but the man kept running. While Wayne continued to pursue the suspect on foot, Henry jumped in his car and kept chase that way. By this time, numerous bystanders had witnessed the pursuit and had called the police. After a lengthy chase and nearly losing him a few times, the man with the knife was soon apprehended. He was identified as twenty-three-year-old George Howard Putt, a young man who had had numerous brushes with the law in the past.

Meanwhile, police had also been summoned to the apartment building on North Bellevue, where the screams had originated. There, the police had found the slashed and mutilated body of Mary Christine Pickens. It was her fifty-ninth birthday.

By that evening, Putt had been arrested and placed in a lineup, where he was identified by only two of eight potential witnesses. Although this was disheartening for the police, luck was on their side. Soon after the lineup, Putt asked to speak to homicide Captain Bob Cochran. When Cochran reached the room where the suspect was being held, Putt simply stated, "I did it. I killed them all." Although the captain had no doubt that Putt was, indeed, guilty, he asked the suspect to elaborate and give him details about the crimes. Putt told him that he would, but that he needed to speak with his wife first.

Officers were soon sent to 624 Bethel Street, where Putt lived with his wife, Mary, and their toddler son, Pip. They informed Mary of her husband's arrest and escorted her down to the police station. When she arrived, she was taken to see her husband. He soon admitted to her that he was the killer. While Mary Putt seemed surprised that her husband was *the* serial killer, she did not seem to have trouble believing that he was capable of such acts. After confessing to his wife, Putt asked her if she thought he should go ahead and confess or not. Mary then wanted to know if there was any evidence linking him to the crimes, and Putt acknowledged that there was. She told him that he might as well confess, then, as they had no money for a lawyer anyway. After spending a little time with his wife, George Putt was led away, and husband and wife were questioned separately.

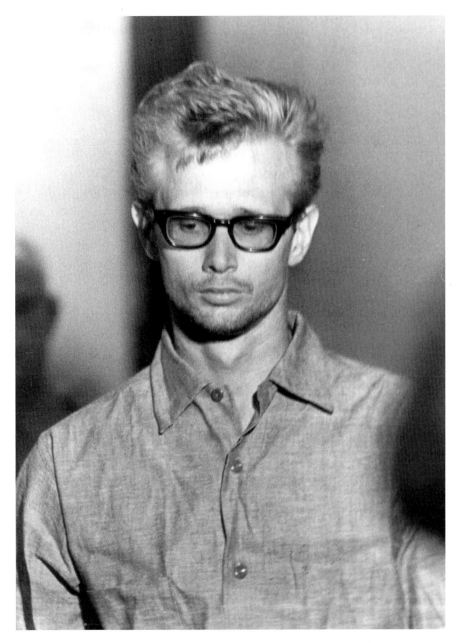

George Howard Putt. *Special Collections, University of Memphis Libraries.*

George Putt had soon confessed to each of the murders in great detail, convincing investigators that he was, indeed, the killer. This detailed confession would also later serve to convince jurors that George Putt had enough intimate knowledge of the crimes to prove that he was the only possible guilty party. The motive for these crimes, he claimed, was simply that he was broke and needed some money. He chose victims that appeared vulnerable and who would likely have cash on them. When asked why he didn't just rob the victims, he simply stated that he couldn't leave any witnesses behind who would send him to prison.

After his confession, Putt was placed in the very same cell of the Shelby County jail that had once held James Earl Ray. More than a year later, Putt was tried for the murder of Mary Christine Pickens in the very same courtroom where James Earl Ray had been tried. Putt's attorneys argued that he was not guilty by reason of insanity. Psychiatrists testifying for the prosecution, however, maintained that Putt was legally sane. On October 27, 1970, the jury found Putt guilty of first-degree murder and the judge sentenced him to death. His attorneys, of course, appealed the conviction, but it was ultimately upheld. In 1972, however, the death penalty was eliminated by the U.S. Supreme Court, which deemed it unconstitutional. Putt's sentence, therefore, was commuted to ninety-nine years, making him eligible for parole after just thirty.

Prosecutors then decided to try Putt for two of the other murders—those of Roy and Bernalyn Dumas. On April 27, 1973, Putt was convicted of two counts of first-degree murder and was sentenced to 199 years in prison for each count. His total sentence for all three counts was 497 years. George Putt is currently serving out his sentence at the Turney Center Industrial Prison in Only, Tennessee. His sentence will officially end on March 1, 2437.

Chapter 14

The Ultimate Betrayal

Rarely does a year go by that we do not hear the story of a child who is left in a car to die in the summer heat. At best, these incidents are caused by a distracted or absent-minded parent or caregiver; at worst, they are caused by a neglectful one who intends to leave the child in the car but does not intend for that child to die. Hardly ever do we hear of a situation in which a living, breathing human being is deliberately placed in the car and left to die in the heat. In 1977, however, that's exactly what happened to one woman. Deborah Groseclose, a twenty-four-year-old mother of two young children, was beaten, stabbed, raped and stuffed in a trunk to die of hyperthermia. The most horrific part of an already horrific story was that her husband paid two men to have it done.

Bill and Deborah Groseclose were married in 1975. Deborah was twenty-two at the time and had a four-year-old daughter named Tonya from a previous marriage. The young bride was a receptionist at a doctor's office, while her husband was a navy recruiter. Shortly after their wedding, the couple bought a house together in the Frayser area, and life seemed good for a while. Before too long, however, Deborah began to see signs of trouble. The couple started having major blowups over seemingly trivial matters. Bill would sometimes go off on bizarre ranting and raving tangents, particularly when he had been drinking. During one especially bad incident when Debbie was three months pregnant, Bill beat his wife severely. Fearing for the life of her unborn child, Deborah immediately left her husband and moved in with her mother. In a short time, though, Bill had convinced her to return home, vowing not to get drunk again. Deborah gave her marriage a valid try, not only for herself, but for her unborn son as well. In July 1976, the Groscloses welcomed that son, Nathan, into the world.

In spite of that happy event, marriage was not blissful for Debbie and Bill. Still, Debbie was determined to give it her best shot because she wanted both Nathan and Tonya to have a family that was intact. It seemed, however, that the effort to save the marriage was somewhat one-sided, as Debbie sometimes went to marriage counseling alone. By the late spring of 1977, she had had enough and had begun to tell her friends that she was going to get a divorce. Meanwhile, Bill had mentioned to at least one of *his* friends that he was never going to be stuck with child support payments again as he was already making payments to one of his previous wives.

On the afternoon of June 28, Debbie was headed to her car after work when a bearded man with reddish hair attempted to stop her. He said that he wanted to talk to her about "her life." Debbie hurriedly got into her car and began driving, but the bearded man followed and continued to follow her all the way home. When she pulled up in her driveway, she began honking the horn and shouting for Bill. When Bill emerged from the house, the car sped off down the road. Debbie reported the incident to the authorities, but her husband never seemed too concerned about it.

The very next morning, Deborah's coworkers became concerned when the young woman did not report for work. They called her home to check on her, but were only able to get a hold of her husband. He was at home taking care of the couple's eleven-month-old son who was ill. Bill told Deborah's coworkers that his wife had been getting ready for work that morning when he ran out to pick up his paycheck. When he returned home, he said, she was already gone.

Playing the role of a concerned husband, Bill asked various neighbors if they had seen his wife that morning, but no one had. He then called his mother-in-law and asked if she had seen Deborah. Deborah's mother, Aline Watts, being familiar with Bill's history of violence toward her daughter, was immediately concerned and insisted that Bill call the police. Because Deborah was a grown woman, however, the police were unable to take a report for seventy-two hours. Meanwhile, Ms. Watts went to the Groseclose home to see for herself that Debbie was gone. She had suspicions that her daughter might have been in the home hurt or being held captive. Though her walk-through of the home revealed nothing, she packed up a few things for Nathan and told Bill she was taking the baby home with her. Bill readily agreed to this suggestion.

When the required seventy-two hours had passed, Deborah's family was finally able to file an official missing person's report with the Memphis Police Department. By then, of course, they were beginning to lose hope that they would ever see Debbie alive again. Though the police were now on the case, Aline Watts and her sister hired a private investigator to try to find Deborah, but no trace of her was uncovered.

Just before noon on July 4, however, the police were called to the main branch of the Memphis Public Library where a suspicious vehicle emitting a strong odor was parked. When the responding officer arrived on the scene, he found a green Plymouth convertible, like the one Debbie drove, parked in the lot with flies swarming around the trunk. When he ran the license plate numbers, he discovered that the car did, indeed, belong to the missing Deborah Groseclose. He immediately called for homicide detectives and a crime scene unit.

Upon opening the trunk of the car, investigators discovered a badly decomposed body that was later positively identified as that of Deborah Groseclose. The autopsy revealed that Deborah had been strangled and stabbed four times in the back. However, that is not what ultimately killed her. It seems that when the young woman was stuffed in the trunk of her own car, she was still alive. In the end, it was hyperthermia that took her life. Later, when the medical examiner was called to testify in court regarding the cause of Deborah Groseclose's death, he explained it this way to the jurors:

The former main branch of the Memphis Public Library. *Memphis and Shelby County Room, Memphis Public Library & Information Center.*

The mechanism of death from systemic hyperthermia is that the body has certain regulatory mechanisms that enable it to keep its body temperature in a certain range. One of those includes the presence of fluids in the body. In an attempt to maintain body temperature in adverse hot environments, the person will sweat and will perspire, and this is significant because the evaporation of water from the body surfaces acts just the same as an air conditioner in that it cools the body.

You can see the same thing if you're hot and sweaty and you stand in front of a fan. You will feel cooler than the normal air temperature around you, and that's because you're evaporating the water much more rapidly. As the body temperature goes up, and as you lose more of the water, eventually you lose so much water that you can no longer properly regulate the body temperature, and the body temperature goes up much more rapidly.

The problem with the body temperature going up is that when you reach a body temperature of about 107.5 degrees Fahrenheit, you start to coagulate the protein in the body. Basically you cook.[15]

After the discovery of Deborah's body, the police launched an intensive investigation into her death. Bill Groseclose, being the spouse of the dead woman, was, of course, high on their list of potential suspects. Investigators began questioning Bill's neighbors and co-workers in an attempt to turn up any detail that might help with the investigation. It didn't take long before they had uncovered at least one potential lead. It was reported that on the day Debbie Groseclose disappeared, a white station wagon had been seen parked at the Groseclose home. When detectives asked Bill to whom the station wagon belonged, he told them that it belonged to an acquaintance of his named Phillip Britt, who had come by to borrow a wrench. The police would soon be speaking with Britt.

In the meantime, another acquaintance of Groseclose came to light after he was spotted at the man's home following Debbie's murder. This man stood out to investigators because he was a bearded man with reddish hair—just like the man that followed Debbie home on the day before she was murdered. The police soon tracked down this bearded man and learned that he was Johnny Townsend. They questioned Townsend casually at first, but felt that he was holding back information. He admitted that he knew Bill Groseclose and further admitted that they had some mutual acquaintances, including Phillip Britt, a man named Ron Rickman and another named Barton Mount. A few days later, the officers returned to Townsend's apartment and asked him specifically if there was something else that he had not told them during the previous interview. Dejected, but apparently eager to get it off his chest, Townsend admitted that he knew a lot more than he had told them and suggested that they go down to the police station so that he could tell his story—one that he gleaned from his roommate, Ron Rickman.

The story began when Bill Groseclose approached his friend Barton Mount and asked him if he would be willing to kill Deborah. Barton said no, but agreed to ask around and see if he could find anyone who would be willing to do so. Groseclose was originally offering to pay a mere $50 for the commission of the crime. Mount approached Phillip Britt, who said he would consider the offer, but complained that $50 was not enough. When Groseclose offered $200 before the murder and $500 after the insurance money came in, Britt was willing to make the deal. He didn't want to do it alone, however, and asked his friend Ron Rickman to assist him. In the end, Britt wanted only to serve as a middleman and did not want to actually commit the murder himself. When all of the details were ironed out, Phillip Britt was to be paid $100 for his part, and Ron Rickman was to be paid $200 up front and $500 after the fact.

Bill Groseclose specified that he wanted the crime to look like a rape-robbery. On the morning of the murder, Bill packed up the baby and left the house at 6:30 a.m., leaving the back door unlocked so that the hired hit men could enter without a problem. Shortly after his departure, Britt and Rickman entered the home and went into the Grosecloses' bedroom, where Deborah was sleeping. She soon woke up with a start and saw Rickman standing there. She cried out for her husband, but of course, he was not there to save her. Rickman ordered her to get undressed and then both he and Britt raped the woman. They then made her bathe and get dressed as if she were going to work. When she was completely ready, Rickman grabbed her from behind and began to strangle her. When he thought she was dead, he released his grip and was shocked when the woman began gasping for air. At that, Rickman took a small knife and stabbed her four times in the back. Then he and Britt dumped her lifeless body into the trunk of her car. They drove her car to the parking lot of the library and discovered that Debbie was still alive and crying for help from the trunk. Convinced that the traffic would drown out her cries, Rickman and Britt simply walked away from the car. It was in that oven of a trunk where Debbie finally died.

After taking Townsend's statement, the police picked up Phillip Britt, Barton Mount, Ron Rickman and Bill Groseclose in for questioning. Of the four men, three of them had soon admitted to their own involvement in the crime, each telling a similar story. The only one who maintained his innocence throughout was Bill Groseclose.

Approximately eight months after Debbie's horrific death, Bill Groseclose, Phillip Britt and Ron Rickman were tried together for her murder. All three were found guilty. Groseclose and Rickman were sentenced to death, while Britt received a life sentence. A 1999 appeal by Groseclose and Rickman, however, resulted in a new trial for the convicted murderers. The 1999 trial upheld the conviction but reduced the men's sentences to life in prison. Having already been denied parole once, both men will be up for parole again in September 2013. Britt will next be eligible for parole in 2011.

Chapter 15

A Murder in Millington

Eighteen-year-old Marine Corps Private Suzanne Marie Collins arrived in Millington on October 20, 1984, to attend Class A avionics school. Suzanne was an enthusiastic and ambitious blonde bombshell with a bright smile and an even brighter future ahead of her. Less than nine months later, however, she would be dead.

As Suzanne settled into life on the naval base, she quickly made a name for herself. She worked hard and pushed herself to exceed the expectations of others. This determination, coupled with her bubbly personality, made her well respected and well loved by most. Her successes, however, were known to occasionally inspire resentment or jealousy among some of her fellow marines. Nevertheless, Suzanne's career and life in general were going well, and by all accounts, she was very happy.

In July 1985, Suzanne and her fellow classmates were scheduled to graduate from avionics school. Although this was a thrilling event for Suzanne, there was one small damper on it. After graduation, Suzanne was being assigned to Marine Corps Air Station Cherry Point, located in Havelock, North Carolina. This wouldn't have been so bad except that her best friend and her boyfriend were both being assigned to posts in California. Suzanne decided that once she began her Cherry Point assignment, she would begin working on getting transferred to California.

Aside from that, however, spirits were high in the days leading up to graduation and Suzanne and her best friend made plans to go out to celebrate on July 11, the night before graduation. At the last minute, however, Suzanne was assigned duty watch in front of the barracks building so she was unable to go. This one small change of plans may have been the very thing that set the events in motion that would ultimately lead to her murder.

Duty watch was a boring and uneventful assignment and as the evening wore on, Suzanne grew restless. At 10:00 pm., finally, her duty was over and she went back to her room. While there, she changed clothes and told her roommates that she was going out for a run. Even at that late hour, no one thought this unusual for Suzanne. She loved to exercise and strived to run several miles each day, in addition to working out in the gym. More importantly, she had been cooped up all evening and was ready to expend a little energy.

At around eleven o'clock that same night, two other marines, Michael Howard and Mark Shotwell, who were out jogging, passed a female marine jogging on the opposite side of the road. Soon after they passed her, they saw a car parked on the shoulder of the road with its headlights on. The car pulled out into the road and drove off in the same direction as the female jogger. Just a moment after the car passed them, Howard and Shotwell heard screams coming from behind them. They immediately turned and ran in the direction of the screams. Just then, they saw the car, a dark-colored Ford station wagon, pull back onto the road.

The two marines lost sight of the car pretty quickly so they ran to the base and reported the incident to a guard there. As it happened, that guard had actually seen the station wagon as it exited through his gate. The guard called base security to report the incident. He described the driver of the vehicle as a male who had his arm around a woman in the passenger seat. He also noted that the car had Kentucky license plates.

A few minutes after midnight, a base watchman spotted a station wagon fitting the description of the car in question and he pulled it over. The car was being driven by a man name Sedley Alley. He was twenty-nine years old and the husband of an enlisted navy woman. Alley's wife, Lynne, roughly matched the description of the possible abduction victim so it was surmised that it had been she riding in the car with him. Sedley Alley was then released. As he drove off in his station wagon, Howard and Shotwell, who were still giving statements, heard the loud muffler of the car and identified it as the car that they had seen earlier in the evening.

At five o'clock on the morning of July 12, one of Suzanne's roommates reported that Suzanne had gone out for a run the night before but had apparently not returned home. When base security obtained photographs of the young woman, they immediately realized she matched the description of the woman seen in Sedley Alley's car and notified area authorities to be on the lookout for the missing marine.

It was just about an hour later when Shelby County sheriff's deputies came across the nude body of a young woman in Edmund Orgill Park in Millington who fit Suzanne Collins's description. The body was badly bruised and bloody, but the most horrific aspect of the body's condition was a tree branch that had been inserted into the vagina. The body was soon identified as that of Suzanne Marie Collins, and Sedley Alley was taken into custody.

The Shelby County medical examiner soon performed an autopsy. Suzanne's cause of death was determined to be:

> *due to multiple injuries inflicted by blunt trauma to the head, pressing on the neck and pushing 20 ½ inches of a 31 inch long, 1 ½ inch diameter sharply beveled tree limb up the perineum through the abdomen into the right chest tearing abdominal and chest organs and producing internal hemorrhaging.*

Back at the base security building, Sedley Alley was relaying his version of the evening's events. He claimed that he had been drinking and accidentally hit Suzanne with his car. He went on to say that he put her in the car to take her to the hospital, but when she awoke, she was in a state of panic. According to this account, he then hit her to shut her up, not thinking about the fact that he held a screwdriver in his hand. Realizing that he had killed her, he then dumped her body at Edmund Orgill Park and staged it to look like a sexual crime by forcing the tree branch into her vagina. After his "confession," Alley led authorities to the tree from where the branch was taken.

The autopsy report did not support Alley's story and soon he was charged with first-degree murder. Almost immediately, the Shelby County assistant district attorney decided that he would push for the death penalty.

On July 18, 1985, Lance Corporal Suzanne Marie Collins was laid to rest at Arlington National Cemetery.

Meanwhile, Sedley Alley had secured legal representation from two of the area's most prominent criminal lawyers. Among the first things they did as Alley's attorneys was have his mental health evaluated. They claimed that their client might possibly suffer from multiple personality disorder. The original trial date was postponed while Alley spent six months being evaluated in a mental hospital. Although no diagnosis was ever made conclusively, it was revealed that while under hypnosis, Alley told of the manifestation of three separate personalities on the night of the murder. While the defense clung to this supposition, the prosecution called in an expert of their own who diagnosed Alley with borderline personality disorder.

Finally, in spite of all of the delays, Sedley Alley went to trial in March 1987. In spite of all the defense's attempts to prove Alley insane, it only took the jury six hours to deliberate. When they returned to the courtroom,

Edmund Orgill Park in Millington. *Teresa R. Simpson.*

A mug shot of Sedley Alley. *Tennessee Department of Corrections.*

they delivered their verdict: Sedley Alley was guilty of first-degree murder, aggravated kidnapping and aggravated rape. It only took the jury two additional hours of deliberation to decide Alley's fate. He was sentenced to death by electrocution. His initial execution date was set for May 2, 1990. He made appeal after appeal, all the while maintaining his multiple personality defense.

In 2004, however, he changed his tactic and declared that he was completely innocent of the crime. He then pushed for DNA testing, asserting that this would clear him of any wrongdoing. As with his other appeals, his push for DNA testing also failed. Again, his execution date was rescheduled, this time for June 28, 2006. By this time, Tennessee was using lethal injection instead of the electric chair for executions.

Just hours before his execution was scheduled, Alley's defense team tried one last-ditch effort to save its client. They hand delivered a final appeal to a judge on the sixth circuit court of appeals at his home. He granted Sedley Alley a stay for the purpose of having DNA analysis done. Almost immediately, however, two other judges reversed the order and the execution was back on.

Just before the lethal drugs were administered, Alley was asked if there was anything he wanted to say. He said, "Yes, to my children. April, David, can you hear me? I love you. Stay strong."[16] With his children watching, Sedley Alley was executed and was pronounced dead at 2:12 a.m. Alley's was Tennessee's first execution in six years and only its second in more than forty-five. Although his attorneys vowed to proceed with DNA testing even after his death, no results of those tests, if performed, have ever been released.

Chapter 16

The West Memphis Three

West Memphis is a small town in Arkansas located just across the Mississippi River from Memphis, Tennessee. With a population of fewer than thirty thousand and a large percentage of those residents falling below the poverty line, the town would probably be considered by many to be unremarkable. Indeed, West Memphis was likely unheard of by most of the nation until the spring of 1993.

On May 5 of that year, three eight-year-old boys disappeared into a neighborhood known as Robin Hood Hills. Steve Branch, Christopher Byers and Michael Moore were seen going into the area at around 6:00 p.m. They never returned.

Christopher's father reported his son's disappearance an hour later, and missing person's reports on the other two boys quickly followed. Although the parents were prompt in notifying the police, one has to wonder if anyone actually suspected that something was seriously wrong at this point. After all, how uncommon could it possibly be for three little boys to wander off for a few hours? Nonetheless, friends, families and neighbors of the boys banded together and conducted a search for the children that very night. This search yielded no trace of them.

The next morning, the police launched an official search. The most thorough search took place in the Robin Hood Hills neighborhood, but no trace of the boys was found all morning. After lunch, however, one searcher discovered a child's shoe in a creek near the Blue Beacon Truck Wash. This creek also led into the Robin Hood Hills neighborhood. After this clue was found, other searchers converged upon the area and made a thorough search of the creek. That is where they came upon a gruesome and heart-wrenching discovery. All three boys were found dead—naked and hogtied—lying in the creek several feet apart. Each of the boys showed signs of having been beaten severely. The autopsy reports painted an even more disturbing picture.

The body of Steve Branch was marred by multiple scratches, cuts and gashes, with the most severe of these on the face and head. The base of the skull had also been fractured, and there were superficial scratches on the penis. Steve Branch's official cause of death was determined to be "multiple injuries with drowning."

The body of Christopher Byers showed the most extensive injuries. Numerous cuts, gashes and abrasions covered the body. The entire genital area appeared to have been mutilated and there were bite marks on the buttocks. In addition, the skull had also been fractured. Christopher Byers's official cause of death was determined to be "multiple injuries."

The body of Michael Moore showed similar, yet somewhat less traumatic injuries, than the body of Steve Branch. Again, there were multiple abrasions, cuts and gashes. The skull was also fractured in two places. And like Steve Branch, Michael Moore's official cause of death was determined to be "multiple injuries with drowning."

It was just one day after the discovery of the bodies that police began speculating about a suspect in the case. One juvenile patrol officer informed investigators that he could think of one person who would have been capable of committing such crimes. That person was Damien Echols.

Damien Echols was born in 1974, and his early childhood was marked by instability. His father's job required the family to make frequent moves, often with very little notice. Eventually, his parents divorced and his mother remarried. Her second husband eventually adopted Damien. During his early teenage years, Damien dabbled in several different religions, including Buddhism, Islam, Catholicism and paganism. He listened to heavy metal bands and read Stephen King novels. He also suffered from bipolar disorder and tried on multiple occasions to commit suicide. At one point, he and a teenage girlfriend ran away from home and broke into a mobile home for shelter during a storm. The police soon arrived and the pair was arrested. That was Damien's first brush with the law. Meanwhile, his home life was deteriorating as his mother and adoptive father were getting divorced. Shortly thereafter, his mother remarried his biological father. Eventually, Damien's mental state improved and he took and passed his GED exam. He also moved in with his girlfriend, who was now pregnant.

When investigators into the boys' murders first looked at Damien Echols, their suspicions were raised by Damien's dabblings into the occult and his preference for heavy metal music. They also investigated many of Damien's friends, including Jason Baldwin. The third suspect in the case, Jessie Misskelley (who had an IQ of seventy-two), came to officials' attention in a convoluted manner. A little boy named Aaron Hutcheson told Marion County police that he knew where the murders took place and even went on to say that the killers were Spanish-speaking Satanists. There was no evidence to support this story, and Aaron was unable to identify Echols or Baldwin in a photo lineup. Aaron's mother, Vicki Hutcheson, allowed the police to wiretap her home, and she agreed to attempt to lure Echols to her house. It was at this point that Jessie Misskelley entered the picture. He sometimes babysat Aaron Hutcheson and therefore knew Vicki Hutcheson relatively well. Vicki asked Jessie if he could get Damien to come over. Although Jessie and Damien were not close friends, the two visited the Hutcheson home together one day. The police were unable to obtain any valuable information from the wiretaps.

Shortly after the wiretap incident, Vicki told authorities that she had attended a Satanic ritual with Damien and Jessie. This convinced investigators that Jessie was also involved in the murders, and they brought him in for questioning. There were multiple discrepancies in Vicki's story and she later recanted her statement. Her recantation came too late to help Jessie, however.

Police questioned Jessie Miskelley for four hours, but less than one hour of the interrogation was tape-recorded. During that time, Jessie confessed to his involvement in the murders. However, his confession was full of erroneous information. Furthermore, experts, including the renowned Dr. Richard Ofshe, would later attest that the confession was a false one, coerced by police officers.[17] In his confession, Jessie made the following incorrect statements: he claimed that the three victims and Jason Baldwin had all skipped school on the day of the murders, when in fact attendance records showed that all four were in school; he said that at least one of the victims was choked to death with a stick, yet the medical examiner found no evidence of strangulation; he said that the victims had been anally raped (a widespread rumor at the time), but there was no forensic evidence to support this; and he also stated that the young boys had been tied up with rope, when in actuality they had been bound with their own shoelaces.

Based primarily on Jessie's confession and on Vicki Hutcheson's statement, Damien Echols and Jason Baldwin were arrested for the murders of Steve Branch, Christopher Byers and Michael Moore. After the arrests, investigators began their searches of Damien's and Jason's homes, uncovering some potentially damning evidence. Clothing similar to that described by Jessie Misskelley was collected, as were fibers from the teenagers' homes. A search of the lake behind Jason's house turned up a survival knife of a similar style as one that Damien had once owned. Damien's journals and other books were collected as evidence, as well. Finally, a necklace belonging to Damien was taken and tested for blood. Specks of blood were found, but in quantities only large enough to determine blood type.

Damien's blood type was identified, as were specks of A+ blood. A+ was both Steve Branch's blood type and Jason Baldwin's. It is also the blood type of approximately 34 percent of the population. As Damien and Jason were known to share the necklace between them, prosecutors decided not to use this evidence at trial.

Due to the lack of forensic evidence, investigators and prosecutors had to focus their attention on witnesses—witnesses either to the crimes themselves, or to discussion of them before or after they took place. One such witness was Parole Officer Jerry Driver. He was the only one to ever come forward who claimed to have seen Damien Echols, Jason Baldwin *and* Jessie Misskelley together at the same time. In spite of his confession, Jessie Misskelley just did not seem to fit into the picture. Another witness was a woman named Narlene Hollingsworth. She and her family were driving down the street on the night of May 5, when she and two of her children reported seeing Damien Echols and his girlfriend, Domini Teer, walking near the Blue Beacon Truck Wash. The rest of the occupants in Narlene's car were unable to verify the sighting, and prosecutors suggested that it was actually Damien walking with Jason Baldwin and *not* Domini Teer that night. Though they were trying to implicate two of the suspects, they did little but create doubt regarding the accuracy of Narlene's testimony.

A final set of three witnesses carried the most impact in the case. Two adolescents—Christy VanVickle, age twelve, and Jackie Medford, age fifteen—reported being at a softball game and overhearing Damien admitting to murdering the three boys. Jackie went on to say that Echols also claimed he was going to kill two more boys before turning himself in. The girls were unable to provide any other details surrounding the conversation, nor were they able to pinpoint the date or time of the softball game in question.

The third witness was a teenager named Michael Carson, who was in the same juvenile detention center as Jason Baldwin. Michael claimed that Jason had confessed to the murders and even went into graphic and gory detail about them. Michael's counselor at the detention center called both the defense and the prosecuting attorneys to inform them that he had been the source of much of Michael's information regarding the case. When the counselor learned that Michael was going to testify that Jason had confessed to him, he further informed attorneys that he believed Michael would be perjuring himself on the stand.

Jessie Misskelley went to trial on January 18, 1994. On February 4, the mentally incompetent boy was found guilty of one count of murder in the first degree and two counts of murder in the second degree. He was sentenced to a term of life plus forty years in prison.

Damien Echols in 2006. *Copyright Grove Pashley, WM3.org, 2008.*

Damien Echols and Jason Baldwin went to trial together on February 22, 1994. On March 19, they were both found guilty of three counts of capital murder. Damien was subsequently sentenced to death by lethal injection, while Jason was sentenced to life in prison without parole.

Jessie Misskelley in 2006. *Copyright Grove Pashley, WM3.org, 2008.*

All of the evidence linking the West Memphis Three to the crimes and presented at trial was circumstantial in nature. Likewise, there was additional circumstantial evidence pointing *away* from Damien, Jason and Jessie.

On the night of May 5, workers at a Bojangles' restaurant (located about a mile from the crime scene), reported than an African American man covered in mud and blood came into the restaurant and went into the women's

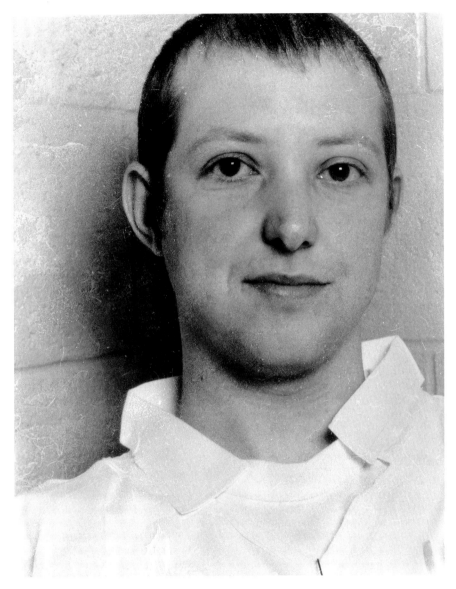

Jason Baldwin in 2006. *Copyright Grove Pashley, WM3.org, 2008.*

restroom. The police were called and an officer responded—*at the drive-through window*—forty-five minutes later. The next day, after the boys' bodies were found, a Bojangles' manager called police again, thinking that there might be a connection between the murders and the bloody man from the night before. Finally, investigators came out and took blood samples from the restroom. Later, however, these samples were lost and testing was never performed on them.

Additional circumstantial evidence pointed to someone who would appear to be an unlikely suspect—John Mark Byers, Christopher Byers's adoptive father. A knife owned by Mr. Byers was found to have bloodstains on it, even though Mr. Byers first claimed the knife had never been used. The bloodstains were of the same type as John Mark and Christopher. No further analysis was done to determine to which of the two they might have belonged.

A black Caucasian hair was found on one of the victims' bodies. This hair was proven to be microscopically similar to that of both Damien Echols and John Mark Byers, but it could not be narrowed down further than that.

John Mark Byers also admitted to having spanked Christopher with a belt prior to his disappearance. This "spanking" left bloody welts on Christopher's buttocks and would probably have rendered him unable to ride his bicycle. Yet John Mark purports that Christopher was riding his bike just hours before his disappearance.

Finally, it is worth noting that John Mark Byers no longer has his teeth. In 1998, he testified that he had lost them as a side effect to taking the drug Tegretol, though such an occurrence is not a commonly cited side effect of the drug. While recent tests have shown that the bite marks on the victims' bodies were not made by Damien, Jason or Jessie, no such comparison could ever be made to the teeth of John Mark Byers.

Fourteen years after the murders, DNA evidence from the crime scene was finally tested. No DNA from Damien Echols, Jason Baldwin, Jessie Misskelley or even John Mark Byers was found. Interestingly enough, however, a hair belonging to Steve Branch's stepfather, Terry Hobbs, was found intertwined in the knots used to bind the three victims. A hearing to present this newfound evidence has been scheduled for late 2008. At least until then, Damien, Jason and Jessie remain in prison, where they have lived nearly half of their young lives.

Conclusion

The sixteen tales of murder and mayhem that you have just read have one predominant underlying theme in common—human nature. The Vadakin and Root slayings were motivated by jealously. The Person and Adams murders were rooted in revenge. The race riot and King assassination were spurred on by hate. And the George Putt and Robin Hood Hills killings were the result of something that can only be described as pure evil. All of these driving forces are nothing more and nothing less than the darker side of human nature.

It is that dark element of human nature that has been the root of all violence since the beginning of time. After all, did not Cain kill his brother Abel in a moment of jealousy? This is not to suggest, of course, that we as people are helpless to prevent violence from happening. It simply means that as long as there are people in the world, there is the *possibility* of violence occurring.

With the preceding accounts of murder in mind, it is worth noting that Memphis alone is not a cesspool of wickedness. No, such atrocities happen everywhere from major metropolises to remote hamlets the world over. Nonetheless, it is true that Memphis is the scene to more than its fair share of murders each year. Is this due to the social and economic dynamics of the population? Is it due to some deficiency within the city government? Could it even be due to something as simple as a lack of moral upbringing? Whatever the cause, it stands to reason that Memphis will continue to be the scene of countless murders for years and generations to come. There will, of course, be those that are forgotten by the conclusion of the evening news and those—even in this city, which some years averages a homicide nearly every other day—that stay etched in our minds forever.

Many of the murders that I hear about on the news or read about in the paper affect me deeply. These crimes are personal because they happen in my hometown. Perhaps murder in Memphis is personal to you, too. Whether you are a former or current resident of the city, a frequent visitor or simply a distant admirer, something prompted you to read about Memphis's murderous past. I hope the journey through this chapter in our history has been an informative and intriguing one, even if not necessarily an uplifting one.

Notes

Chapter 1

1. "Reports of Outrages, Riots and Murders, Jan. 15, 1866–Aug. 12, 1868," *Freedmen's Bureau*, April 15, 2008, http://freedmensbureau.com/tennessee/outrages/memphisriot.htm.

Chapter 2

2. "Wages of Sin," *New York Times*, September 4, 1871, 1.
3. Ibid.
4. "The Last Memphis Murder," *New York Herald*, September 6, 1871, 8.

Chapter 3

5. "Godwin on Trial," *New York Times*, January 26, 1887.

Chapter 4

6. "Jealousy the Motive: A Strange Story Told by the Memphis Girl Murderer," *New York Times*, January 29, 1892, 1.

Chapter 6

7. "Accused of Murder," *Delphos* [Ohio] *Daily Herald*, May 15, 1903, 1.

CHAPTER 10

8. Michael Finger, "Murder in Memphis," *Memphis,* March 2002, 52.

9. "Forgiving Father," *TIME*, December 2, 1935.

CHAPTER 11

10. Ruth Reynolds, "Justice is Aroused to Pity by Miserable Target of Poverty," *Post-Standard* [Syracuse], July 3, 1949, 13.

11. "Mrs. Gill Confident of Acquittal If Jury 'Ignores My Past,'" *Delta Democrat-Times* [Greenville, MS], January 20, 1949, 8

CHAPTER 12

12. "King Challenges Court Restraint, Vows to March," *Commercial Appeal* [Memphis], April 4, 1968.

13. Branch, *At Canaan's Edge*, 766.

14. Mark Gribben, "James Earl Ray: The Man Who Killed Dr. Martin Luther King, Jr." *Crime Library*, April 2, 2008, http://www.crimelibrary. com/terrorists_spies/assassins/ray/1.html.

CHAPTER 14

15. *State of Tennessee v. Ronald Eugene Rickman and William Edward Groseclose*, No. W1999-01744-CCA-R3-CD (Tennessee Court of Criminal Appeals 2002, 2008), www.tsc.state.tn.us/OPINIONS/TCCA/PDF/022/ grosecl.pdf.

CHAPTER 15

16. "Tenn. Executes 2nd Person In 45 Years," *CBS News*, April 29, 2008.

CHAPTER 16

17. James Morgan, "John Grisham, Meet Dan Stidham," *Arkansas Times,* May 1996.

Bibliography

"Avenged His Sister." *Mitchell Daily Republican*, December 7, 1886.

Barron, James. "Percy Foreman, Texas Lawyer, 86; Defended the Assassin of Dr. King." *New York Times*, August 26, 1988.

Branch, Taylor. *At Canaan's Edge: America in the King Years, 1965–68*. New York: Simon & Schuster, 2007.

Douglas, John, and Mark Olshaker. *Journey Into Darkness*. New York: Scribner, 1997.

Dreier, Peter. "Why He Was in Memphis." *American Prospect*, January 15, 2007.

Finger, Michael. "Death in August." *Memphis*, July/August 2005.

"Ford Plant Bandits Kill 3, Wound 4." *New York Times*, August 11, 1921.

"Godwin as a Lover." *Atlanta Constitution*, February 7, 1887.

Johnson, James Weldon, and Sondra K. Wilson, eds. *The Selected Writings of James Weldon Johnson*. Vol. II. New York: Oxford University Press, 1995.

King, Dr. Martin Luther. "I've Been to the Mountaintop." April 3, 1968. Mason Temple. Memphis, Tennessee.

Lovett, Bobby. "Memphis Race Riot of 1866." *The Tennessee Encyclopedia of History and Culture*, March 26, 2008. http://tennesseeencyclopedia.net/imagegallery.php?EntryID=M080.

"Memphis May 22, A.D., 1917." Supplement to *The Crisis* (July 1917).

"The Memphis Riot Investigation." *New York Times*, June 7, 1866.

"The Memphis Riots." *Harper's Weekly*, May 26, 1866.

Meyer, Gerald. *The Memphis Murders*. New York: Seabury Press, 1974.

"MPD History." *Memphis Police Department* Online. April 24, 2008. http://memphispolice.org/History%202004.htm.

"Negro is Burned by Memphis Mob." *Fort Wayne News*, May 22, 1917.

Porch, Dorris D., and Rebecca Easley. *Murder in Memphis*. Far Hills, NJ: New Horizon Press, 1997.

"Release Negroes; Mob Fades Away." *Sandusky Star Journal*, May 23, 1917.

"Rush Memphis Trial in Ford Plant Hold-Up." *New York Times*, August 13, 1921.

Tennessee Lawman Homepage. April 28, 2008. www.tennesseelawman. com/9-fallen.

"Think Same Slayer Killed Two Couples." *New York Times*, May 25, 1923.

"Tragedy Rivals Molineux Case." *Lincoln Evening News*, May 14, 1903.

Wells, Homer G. "The Capture of the Memphis Terror." *True Detective Mysteries*, December 1925.

William, Frederick. *History of the Arkansas Press for a Hundred Years and More.* Little Rock: Parke-Harper Publishing Company, 1922.

"Woman Involved in 3 Mates' Deaths Dies." *Corpus Christi Times*, October 16, 1970.

About the Author

Teresa R. Simpson was born and raised in Memphis, Tennessee, where she lives with her husband and children. As a freelance writer, she has written numerous articles on her hometown for About.com, as well as articles and essays on a variety of subjects for other print and online publications. Teresa is also the author of *The Everything Baby Sign Language Book*, published by Adams Media in 2008.

Visit us at
www.historypress.net